Common Core Support Coach

TARGET Reading Comprehension 2

Common Core Support Coach, Target: Reading Comprehension, First Edition, Grade 2
T355NA ISBN-13: 978-1-62928-315-9
Cover Design: Q2A/Bill Smith **Cover Illustration:** Aga Kowalska/The Organisation

Triumph Learning® 136 Madison Avenue, 7th Floor, New York, NY 10016

Printed in the United States of America. 10 9 8

Contents

Literature

Common Core State Standards

Informational Text

Lesson 1

Stories

When you read a **story**, you read made-up events with made-up characters. In this lesson, you will read three stories about characters with problems.

Skills Focus

- Story Structure
- Context Clues
- Ask and Answer Questions
- Character's Response
- Dictionaries
- Illustrations

Story Structure

Most stories have a beginning, a middle, and an ending. **Story structure** shows how these parts work together to tell a story.

Let's Try It

Read this story.

Azim was at the playground. He looked up at a big tree. His soccer ball was caught in the branches!

Azim threw his hat at the ball. The ball did not come down. Then Azim found a long stick. He poked the ball with the stick.

The ball fell into Azim's hands!

What is the problem at the beginning of the story? Underline the text that tells you.

Discuss What events happen in the middle of the story? Which event solves Azim's problem at the end?

Context Clues

Context clues help you figure out the meaning of a word you do not know. Context clues may be words in the same sentence or words in a sentence close to the unknown word.

Let's Try It Read these sentences.

"Your mother told me that you like baseball," said Mrs. Pine. "So I brought my **equipment**. I have a glove, a bat, and a ball!"

To learn what *equipment* means, look for context clues that show what Mrs. Pine brought. Underline the context clues for *equipment*.

Practice

Use context clues to figure out the meaning of the words below in **bold print**. Underline the context clues that helped you. Circle the meaning of the word in **bold print**.

1. She **whipped** the ball to Jaime. It flew fast and hit his glove with a loud *thwack*.

   threw hard   threw lightly

2. Then Mrs. Pine gave Jaime some batting tips. Jaime **smacked** the ball over her head!

   threw   hit

Read for a Purpose

1 1st Reading

2 2nd Reading

3 3rd Reading

Read along with your teacher. Each time, read for a different purpose. Use the Tools on pages 33 and 34 as you read.

Learning Something New

What is Jaime's problem at the beginning of the story? Underline the words that help you know.

When does this story take place? Circle the text that tells you.

Jaime liked to play baseball.

Mom usually took him to the park to play every Saturday. On this Saturday, Mom had a meeting. So Mom wanted Jaime to go to the park with Mrs. Pine. She was a neighbor. Jaime didn't like this idea.

"This is going to be boring," Jaime thought to himself.

There was a knock at the front door. It was Mrs. Pine. Mom opened the door and called back inside to Jaime.

"Listen to Mrs. Pine," Mom said. "You might learn something new! See you later!"

A moment later, Mrs. Pine walked into the kitchen. She was wearing a baseball glove. She had a bat and a ball, too. Jaime tried not to roll his eyes at her.

"Your mother told me that you like baseball," said Mrs. Pine. "So I brought my **equipment**. I have a glove, a bat, and a ball!"

Jaime shook his head. "This is going to be boring," he thought again.

What does Jaime think when he first meets Mrs. Pine? Circle the text that helps you know.

Why does Mom tell Jaime he might learn something new?

What is the setting in the middle of the story? Circle the text that tells you.

Why is Jaime glad that no one is at the field?

The field was empty when they got to the park. Jaime felt glad.

"Let's warm up first," Mrs. Pine said. She put on her glove.

"I bet she can't even throw far," Jaime thought.

"Are you ready?" Mrs. Pine yelled. She **whipped** the ball to Jaime. It flew fast and hit his glove with a loud *thwack*.

"Wow! She's good," thought Jaime. "This isn't so boring!"

Mrs. Pine saw that Jaime was surprised. "I played softball when I was in school," Mrs. Pine said.

"Can you teach me to throw like that?" Jaime asked.

"Sure!" she said.

Mrs. Pine showed him how to set his feet. Then she showed him how to wind up and snap his wrist. Soon Jaime could **hurl** the ball faster than he had ever thrown it before.

"This is not boring at all!" he thought. "It's fun!"

What events make Jaime think "This is not boring at all!"? Underline the text that helps you know.

How have Jaime's feelings changed from the beginning to the ending of the story? Underline the words that help you know Jaime's feelings.

Then Mrs. Pine gave Jaime some batting tips. Jaime **smacked** the ball over her head!

"Wow!" said Mrs. Pine. "You're a good hitter!"

Mrs. Pine looked at her watch. "We should go now," she said.

At home, Mom asked what they had done all morning.

"We had fun!" said Mrs. Pine with a smile.

"We sure did!" said Jaime. "I listened to Mrs. Pine, and it wasn't boring at all!"

Check off after each reading. 1st Reading 2nd Reading 3rd Reading

✔ Ask and Answer Questions

You can ask **questions** about a story as you read. Then you can look for the **answers** in the text.

Let's Try It Read this story.

Elena heard a knock on the apartment door. It was her new babysitter.

"Yuck," thought Elena. "I don't want a new babysitter!"

A woman walked into the living room. She looked friendly. Best of all, she carried a big box of art supplies.

Elena smiled. She loved to make things!

Who is this story about? Underline the text that tells you the answer. Where does the story take place? Double underline the text that tells you.

Discuss How does Elena feel at the end of the story? How do you know?

Comprehension Check

1. What events happen in the middle of the story?

2. How is Jaime's problem solved by the end of the story?

3. Read this sentence from the story.

   Soon Jaime could <u>hurl</u> the ball faster than he had ever thrown it before.

   Circle the word that helps you understand the meaning of the word *hurl*. Then write the meaning of the word.

Respond to Text: Analyze

Jaime thinks Mrs. Pine will be boring. What does Jaime learn when he has fun with her? Use the information from the text to analyze what Jaime learns.

Let's Try It Make a list of what Jaime learns from his morning with Mrs. Pine. List four things he learns that are NOT about baseball.

What Jaime Learns

On Your Own

Write a short paragraph that tells what Jaime learns from his morning with Mrs. Pine. Support your answer with details. Use what you wrote on this page and in your Tools on pages 33–34.

✓ Character's Response

In stories, we read what a character does, says, thinks, and feels. These actions, words, thoughts, and feelings are how the character **responds** to events and challenges, or problems the character has in the story.

Let's Try It Read this story.

Magda lost her backpack. All day, she looked for it. She looked in her closet. She looked in the kitchen. She even looked in her family's car. The backpack was gone.

"I know!" said Magda. She took the cover off an old pillow. She put her books inside the cover.

"Perfect!" she said. Then she went to school.

What problem does Magda have to solve? Underline the text that tells you. How does Magda respond to her problem? Double underline the text that tells you.

Discuss What does Magda do to solve her problem? What does this tell you about her?

Dictionaries

A **dictionary** is a book or a website that gives the meanings of words. You can use a dictionary to find the meanings of words you cannot figure out on your own.

Let's Try It Read the sentences and the dictionary entries.

"That's a great idea," Charles said. "Mom can be our **customer**."

cus•tom•er (kus'-tə-mər) *noun.* a person who buys things at a store

cut (kut) *verb.* to split something into two pieces with a sharp tool

Circle the entry that tells you the meaning of *customer.*

Practice

Use a dictionary to find the meaning of the word in **bold print** in each sentence below. Circle the meaning that is closest to the definition in the dictionary.

1. They put boxes together to make a **counter**.

   a flat surface   a store

2. Then they **groomed** the animals with a brush.

   painted   cleaned

Read for a Purpose

1 1st Reading

2 2nd Reading

3 3rd Reading

Read along with your teacher. Each time, read for a different purpose. Use the Tools on pages 35 and 36 as you read.

The Pet Shop Mystery

What does Sophie do because she is tired of playing games? Underline the text that helps you know.

Look at the illustration. What clues help you know how Sophie and Charles feel?

Rain hit the living room window. Inside on the couch, Sophie and Charles were tired of playing games. They needed something fun to do.

Sophie came up with an idea. She pointed to Charles's pets.

"You have three pets in your home," she said. "We can open a pretend pet shop!"

"That's a great idea," Charles said. "My mom can be our **customer**."

Sophie and Charles got to work. First they made a **counter**.

"Now we need a sign for our pet shop," Charles said.

"The name needs to be something really special," said Sophie.

"We can call it Pet Paradise!" Charles said.

"Great idea!" said Sophie. "You're very creative."

Charles got his pets. He put them all on the counter. First, he got Racer the rabbit. Next, he got Ham the hamster. Finally, he picked up his huge cat, Spike. Spike was heavy!

How does Sophie respond to Charles's idea for the name of the pet shop? Underline the text that helps you know.

How does the illustration help you understand what a counter is?

Look at the illustration. How do you know Racer might get out of the cage?

Sophie and Charles made signs for the pets. Then they **groomed** the animals with a brush. Spike rolled around on the floor. Ham squeaked, and Racer sniffed the brush.

After that they fed treats to the pets. Spike got cat treats. Ham got lettuce. Racer ate carrots.

Charles tried to sell a pet to Mom. Mom couldn't decide which one to buy.

"Racer is soft and cuddly," said Sophie. "Spike is so cute. He'd make a great feline friend."

"Why don't we have a snack while I decide?" Mom said.

After eating, Charles and Sophie returned to the living room. The door of Racer's cage was wide open. Racer was gone!

"I forgot to lock Racer's cage!" said Sophie. "We have to find her!"

"Now we have to be pet **detectives**," Charles said. "What should we do first?"

"Let's look in the garden!" said Sophie. "The door to the outside is open."

They ran into the garden. The rain had stopped. But Racer wasn't anywhere in the yard.

At first, how do the children respond to losing Racer? Underline the text that helps you know. What does that tell you about them?

What might have happened if Sophie had forgotten to lock Ham the hamster's cage?

How does Sophie know where to find Racer? Underline details that help you know. What does that tell you about her?

Why is Sophie a very good pet detective?

Charles and Sophie ran back inside. They were really worried.

"Wait!" cried Sophie. "Let's follow this trail!" She pointed to the carrots on the floor.

Charles smiled when he saw what Sophie meant. They crouched down to get a better look. There was Racer!

"I think we solved our first case," said Sophie.

"Maybe we make better pet detectives than pet shop owners," Charles said.

Check off after each reading.

1st Reading 2nd Reading 3rd Reading

Illustrations

Illustrations are drawings or photographs that you see in a story. Illustrations help you understand the events and characters in the story.

Let's Try It Look at the illustration.

What game are these two girls playing? Draw a box around a clue that helps you know. Where are they? Circle details that help you know the setting.

Discuss How do the two girls feel? What details in the illustration are clues that help you know this?

Comprehension Check

1. How do Sophie and Charles respond when they do not find Racer in the garden?

2. Look at the illustration on page 21. What details give you clues about where Racer might be?

3. Read these sentences from the story.

   "I think we solved our first case," said Sophie.

   "Maybe we make better pet detectives than pet shop owners," Charles said.

noun. a person who finds clues to solve mysteries

   Circle the word in the **bold print** sentences that matches the meaning shown in the dictionary entry. Then use that word in another sentence.

Respond to Text: Compare and Contrast

"Learning Something New" and "The Pet Shop Mystery" are both stories. You **compare** them by looking at how they are the same. You **contrast** them by looking at how they are different.

Let's Try It What is the same about the **characters** in both stories? What is different?

Jaime	Jaime, Sophie, and Charles	Sophie and Charles

On Your Own

Write a short paragraph that tells how the characters in "Learning Something New" and "The Pet Shop Mystery" are the same. Tell how they are different, too. Support your answer with details from the chart above and from your Tools on pages 33–36.

Take-Home Book

1. Remove this story from your book.
2. Read it three times. Use what you have learned about stories.

1 1st Reading	Story Structure
2 2nd Reading	Character's Response
3 3rd Reading	Critical Thinking

3. Answer the questions in the Comprehension Check on page 32.

Name: ____________________

Read for a Purpose

Read the text three times. Use the skills you have learned. Then complete the Comprehension Check.

1 1st Reading
Story Structure

2 2nd Reading
Character's Response

3 3rd Reading
Critical Thinking

Skunk and the Big Tree

Skunk and Mouse were friends. But they were very different.

Skunk didn't want to climb to the tops of trees. Mouse did. Skunk didn't want to dive into a pile of leaves. Mouse did.

Most of all, Skunk didn't want to walk across the big tree that crossed the river. Mouse always did. Mouse was brave. Skunk was not.

"You can do it," Mouse told Skunk.

Skunk said, "No. No, I can't do it!"

What problem does Skunk have at the beginning of the story? Underline two sentences that tell you. One sentence has been underlined for you.

"It's easy," said Mouse. "Watch me."

Mouse scampered across the big tree.

Suddenly, a few raindrops fell from the sky.

"Come to my house, Skunk," Mouse called. "Get out of the rain!"

Mouse's house was across the river.

Skunk said, "No. No, I can't do it!"

Then rain poured out of the sky.

Skunk got his raincoat. Then he noticed something scary. The rain made the river rise higher and higher.

Suddenly, the rushing water pushed the big tree in front of Mouse's house. The tree blocked Mouse's door!

"Should I go across?" said Skunk. "No. No, I can't do it!"

What does Skunk do when he sees that the tree has blocked Mouse's door? Circle details that help you know.

Would Skunk have crawled across the tree if another animal were in trouble? Why or why not?

Soon the rain stopped. Mouse tried to open the door, but it wouldn't **budge**.

"Help!" Mouse yelled.

How could Skunk help? He would have to walk across the tree!

Skunk looked at the tree. Then he thought about his friend. She was in trouble!

Then he said, "I can fix this. I know I can."

What problem does Skunk solve at the end of the story? Underline the details that help you know.

Skunk climbed on the big tree. The sound of the water roared in his ears. The loud roar made him shake even more. He crawled slowly.

Before long, he was on the other side!

"Don't worry, Mouse!" he yelled. "I'll help you!" Skunk dug and dug and made a tunnel. He got Mouse out!

"Skunk, you are very brave," Mouse said.

"Yes. Yes, I am," said Skunk.

How does Skunk move across the tree? Circle the text that helps you know. What does this tell you about Skunk?

Check off after each reading.

1st Reading 2nd Reading 3rd Reading

Comprehension Check

1. Why does Skunk say, "I can fix this"?

2. Look at the two illustrations on page 31. How does each illustration show you how Skunk feels?

3. Read this sentence from the story.

   Mouse tried to open the door, but it wouldn't budge.

   Circle the word or words that help you understand the meaning of the word *budge*. Then write the meaning of *budge*.

Name: ______________________________

Learning Something New

1 1st Reading **Story Structure**

Page 8

Beginning

Page 11

Middle

Page 12

Ending

Name: ______________________________

Learning Something New

2 2nd Reading Ask and Answer Questions

Page 8: The story takes place on

______________________________.

Page 9: When Jaime first meets Mrs. Pine, he thinks

______________________________.

Page 10: The setting in the middle of the story is

______________________________.

3 3rd Reading Critical Thinking

Page 9: Mom tells Jaime he might learn something new because

____

______________________________.

Page 10: Jaime is glad no one is at the field because

____

______________________________.

Name: ____________________

The Pet Shop Mystery

1 1st Reading Character's Response

What Happens	How Character Responds
Page 18: Sophie is tired of playing games.	Sophie . . .
Page 19: Charles says they should name the pet shop Pet Paradise.	Sophie . . .
Page 21: The children discover that Racer is gone.	Sophie and Charles . . .
Page 22: Sophie sees the carrots.	Sophie . . .

Name: ______________________________

The Pet Shop Mystery

2 2nd Reading Illustrations

Page 18: The illustration shows that the children feel ______________

because ______________________________.

Page 19: The illustration shows that a counter is ______________

______________________________.

Page 20: I know Racer might get out of the cage because

____

______________________________.

3 3rd Reading Critical Thinking

Page 21: If Sophie forgot to lock Ham's cage, ______________

____

______________________________.

Page 22: Sophie is a very good pet detective because ______________

____

______________________________.

Lesson 2

Fables

A **fable** is a story that teaches a lesson about life. You will read three fables. Each one has a moral, or lesson, that you can connect to your own life.

Skills Focus

- Character's Response
- Roots and Prefixes
- Central Message
- Story Structure
- Roots and Suffixes
- Retell Stories

Character's Response

A **character** is a person or an animal in a story. We know how characters **respond** to story events by reading what they do, say, think, and feel.

Let's Try It Read this story.

The Fox and the Grapes

One day, Fox saw a bunch of grapes hanging high on a vine. "I can reach those sweet grapes," he said. "Then I will have a tasty treat."

Fox jumped and jumped. But he could not reach the grapes.

"Those grapes must be sour," Fox grumbled as he slunk away.

Underline what Fox does in the story. Double underline what Fox says about the grapes.

Discuss Why does Fox say the grapes are sweet? Why does he say they are sour?

✓ Roots and Prefixes

A **prefix** is a word part that is added to the beginning of a root word. Adding a prefix to a root word creates a new word with a new meaning.

The prefix *un-* means "not."

The prefix *re-* means "again."

Let's Try It

Read the root word. What does it mean? Now add the prefix. What is the meaning of the new word?

Prefix	Root Word	New Word	Meaning
un-	kind	unkind	not kind
re-	heat	reheat	heat again

Practice

Read each sentence below. Circle the prefix in each underlined word. Then read the two meanings below the sentence. Circle the correct meaning of the word.

1. My friends are <u>unable</u> to visit me this afternoon.

   not able   able to come again

2. We can <u>reuse</u> our bags the next time we go shopping.

   not use   use again

Read for a Purpose

1 1st Reading

2 2nd Reading

3 3rd Reading

Read along with your teacher. Each time, read for a different purpose. Use the Tools on pages 65 and 66 as you read.

Han-shin and the Bowl of Rice

based on a Chinese fable

Han-shin's family is poor. Underline what Han-shin does for his family.

Long ago there lived a boy named Han-shin. Han-shin's family was very poor. They had no money and very little to eat.

Every day, Han-shin went to the river to fish. He wanted to help his family get food. But no matter how hard he tried, he was **unable** to catch a fish. So he and his family went hungry.

Every day, a few women also came to the river. There they washed their dirty clothes. One kind old woman saw that poor Han-shin looked **unhappy**.

"That boy is as skinny as a stick," the old woman said. "He must be very hungry."

The old woman wanted to help Han-shin. "Here," she said to him. "Take this bowl of rice. You look like you have not eaten in a long time."

Han-shin was grateful for the rice. "Thank you," he told the woman. He gobbled down a few bites of rice. Then he wrapped the rest in his shirt. "I will bring the rest home to my family," he told the old woman.

Underline what the woman does for Han-shin. Double underline how Han-shin responds to her.

What happens at the river? Why are these events important?

Han-shin takes some of the rice home. How do you think the old woman feels about that?

The old woman brings Han-shin rice every day. What does Han-shin promise to do for her?

Every day after that, the old woman gave Han-shin a bowl of rice to eat.

"You are very kind," Han-shin told the old woman. "When I grow up, I will find a way to **repay** you for your kindness."

Years passed. Han-shin got bigger and stronger. He grew up and joined the king's army. He became the king's bravest and strongest warrior. As a reward, the king gave Han-shin gold. He gave Han-shin a palace to live in, too. Han-shin and his family would never be hungry again.

Han-shin had everything he could want. But he never forgot the promise he made to the old woman. He would not be truly happy until he **repaid** her.

Han-shin looked all over the kingdom for the old woman. He traveled east and west. He traveled north and south. At last he found her. She was very old.

"I have been looking far and near for you," Han-shin said. "Come with me to my palace."

At the palace, Han-shin **removed** his helmet and **untied** his cape. "I remember how you helped me," he said. "I have not forgotten my promise to pay back your kindness."

Han-shin gave the woman a bowl filled with gold.

What is important to Han-shin now that he is grown up? Circle his words that tell you.

How does the old woman respond to the gold? What do Han-shin and the old woman do next?

Circle the message, or moral, of this story. How do you know that Han-shin has learned this lesson?

Why does the old woman stay at the palace?

"Thank you," said the old woman. "But I cannot take your gold. I only gave you bowls of rice. You have become a kind man. That was my one wish. You have already repaid me."

"If you do not take my gold," Han-shin said, "then you must stay here with my family. We will take care of you forever. Please accept my offer to you. Even a small gift should be repaid with great kindness."

The old woman could not say no to his generosity. Han-shin was true to his word. He took care of her for the rest of her life.

Check off after each reading. 1st Reading 2nd Reading 3rd Reading

Central Message

The lesson in a story is called its **central message**. A message is what you learn from the story. In a fable, this message is called the **moral** of the story.

Let's Try It Read this story.

The Bundle of Sticks

A father found his four sons quarreling. He had one son bring him a bundle of sticks. He asked each son to break the bundle. But none of them could do it.

The father untied the bundle. He gave each son one stick to break. They quickly broke every stick. The father said, "My sons, these sticks are stronger together than apart. And so are you."

Circle the message, or moral of the story. Underline the text that helps you understand the message.

Discuss Look at the text you underlined. How does it help you understand the central message?

Comprehension Check

1. Han-shin responds to gifts by sharing them. Give two examples from the story that show this.

2. What does Han-shin mean when he says that even a small gift should be repaid with kindness?

3. Read this sentence from the story.

   One kind old woman saw that poor Han-shin looked unhappy.

   Circle the prefix in the underlined word. Then write the meaning of the word.

Respond to Text: Compare

You compare two or more things to find out how they are alike. You can compare characters, events, settings, or ideas in stories.

Let's Try It List details about the gifts that the old woman and Han-shin give each other.

The Old Woman's Gift	Han-shin's Gift

On Your Own

Write a short paragraph that tells how the two gifts in "Han-shin and the Bowl of Rice" are alike. Support your answer with details. Use what you wrote on this page and in your Tools on pages 65–66.

Story Structure

Most stories have a beginning, a middle, and an ending. **Story structure** is how these parts work together to tell a story.

Let's Try It Read these paragraphs.

One dry day, a thirsty crow needed water. He found a tall pitcher with some water in it. But the water was too low for him to drink.

The crow picked up some small stones. He dropped the stones into the pitcher one by one. Each stone made the water rise a little bit.

Underline what the beginning of the story tells you. Double underline what the crow does to try and solve the problem.

Discuss What details do you look for at the beginning of a story? Tell what part of this story is missing and what you think will happen in that part.

Roots and Suffixes

A **suffix** is a word part that is added to the end of a root word. Adding a suffix to a root word creates a new word with a new meaning.

The suffix -*ful* means "full of."

The suffix -*less* means "without."

Let's Try It

Read the root word. What does it mean? Now add the suffix. What is the meaning of the new word?

Suffix	Root Word	New Word	Meaning
-ful	fear	fearful	full of fear
-less	fear	fearless	without fear

Practice

Read the first pair of sentences. Circle a suffix and add it to the underlined word. Write the new word in the second sentence. Make sure each sentence tells the same idea. Repeat with the second pair of sentences.

1. I like to <u>help</u>. **ful** **less**

   I try to be ______________ to my mom.

2. We cannot <u>use</u> that broken hammer. **ful** **less**

   That hammer is ______________.

Read for a Purpose

1 1st Reading

2 2nd Reading

3 3rd Reading

Read along with your teacher. Each time, read for a different purpose. Use the Tools on pages 67 and 68 as you read.

Not So Clever Fox

based on a Romanian fable

Underline the characters. What does the beginning of the story tell you they are going to do?

One day, Fox was on his way to the farmer's chicken coop. Along the way, he met Hedgehog.

"Where are you going?" Hedgehog asked.

"I'm going to get a chicken for my lunch," Fox said.

"Aren't you afraid of the farmer?" Hedgehog asked.

"I'm **fearless**," said Fox. "And I'm too clever for the farmer. Come with me. I will show you how easy it is. I have done it before."

Hedgehog was also clever, but he was not **boastful**. "Be **careful**," Hedgehog said to Fox. "I don't think the farmer will let you in again so easily."

"Don't worry," said Fox. "I know my business. Just come with me."

Hedgehog went with Fox.

But just as Hedgehog had said, the clever farmer was prepared. He knew where Fox had squeezed in the last time. Just in that spot, the farmer had dug a deep pit. As Fox and Hedgehog sneaked in, the pair of them tumbled to the bottom of the pit.

Underline the problem in the story. Which part of the story tells about the problem?

Retell the beginning of the story in your own words.

Why does Hedgehog say that the farmer will not let Fox in again so easily this time?

What does Hedgehog do to solve his problem? What problem does Fox still have?

Hedgehog turned to Fox. "I thought you were such a clever fellow," he said. "I warned you."

"What good is talking now?" replied Fox. "We must figure out how to get out of this pit fast." Fox was scared that the farmer would soon come back.

The two of them thought and thought. Then Hedgehog had a clever idea. "I don't feel well," he said with a sneaky smile. "My stomach is upset. I think I'm going to be sick."

"What!" cried Fox. "Not in here with me! Out you go!"

Fox grabbed Hedgehog and tossed him out.

As soon as he got out, Hedgehog chuckled. "I thought you were so clever, Fox. But you are still in the pit, and I am not!"

Fox felt **helpless**. "Have pity on me," he said. "Please help me get out, too."

"Okay," said Hedgehog. "I have a plan. You play dead. When the farmer finds you, he will pick you up and toss you out."

What does Fox ask Hedgehog to do? How does Hedgehog help Fox? What part of the story is this?

Retell the middle of the story in your own words.

How is Fox's problem solved at the end?

Retell the end of the story in your own words.

Do you think Fox will be more or less boastful now? Why?

Fox was **hopeful** about this plan. He did just what Hedgehog told him.

When the farmer came and peered down, he saw Fox playing dead. He grabbed Fox and threw him out of the pit. Quicker than you could clap your hands, Fox was on his feet and running away.

Hedgehog waited nearby for Fox. "I may be clever," the **cheerful** Fox told him. "But not as clever as you, Hedgehog."

Since that day, Fox and Hedgehog have been great friends.

Check off after each reading.

1st Reading

2nd Reading

3rd Reading

✓ Retell Stories

To **retell** means to "tell again." When you retell a story, you tell about its beginning, middle, and end. You use your own words to tell about the setting, characters, and events.

Let's Try It Read this story.

One day, a village boy who herded the sheep cried, "Wolf! Wolf! Help me!" The villagers came running. But they found no wolf. The boy laughed at his joke.

The boy played his trick a few times. Each time, the villagers came. Then one day, a wolf came! The boy cried "Wolf! Wolf! Help me!" But this time, no one came to help.

Read this sentence.

The boy tricked the villagers more than once.

Circle the sentences in the story that the sentence in **bold print** retells.

Discuss Retell this story to a partner. Discuss the lesson, or moral, of the story.

Comprehension Check

1. How do the events on page 54 help end the story?

2. Read these sentences from the story.

"What good is talking now?" replied Fox.

Fox grabbed Hedgehog and tossed him out.

Circle the sentence that tells a detail you would use to retell the story. Then write why.

3. Read these sentences from the story.

Fox felt helpless. "Have pity on me," he said. "Please help me get out, too."

Circle the suffix in the underlined word. Then write the meaning of the word.

Respond to Text: Compare and Contrast

Both "Han-shin and the Bowl of Rice" and "Not So Clever Fox" are fables. Each one has a moral. You can compare and contrast the morals the same way you would compare other parts of the stories.

Let's Try It

Compare and contrast the morals of the fables.

"Han-shin and the Bowl of Rice"	"Not So Clever Fox"
Moral: Even a small gift should be repaid with great kindness.	**Moral:** Do not think you are more clever than anyone else.

On Your Own

Write a short paragraph telling which moral you think is more helpful and why. Support your answer with details. Use what you wrote on this page and in your Tools on pages 65–68.

Take-Home Book

1. Remove this fable from your book.

2. Read it three times. Use what you have learned about fables.

   1 1st Reading Story Structure

   2 2nd Reading Character's Response

   3 3rd Reading Critical Thinking

3. Answer the questions in the Comprehension Check on page 64.

Name: ______________________________

Read for a Purpose

1 1st Reading
Story Structure

2 2nd Reading
Character's Response

3 3rd Reading
Critical Thinking

Read the text three times. Use the skills you have learned. Then complete the Comprehension Check.

The Honest Woodcutter

based on a French fable

Once there lived a poor woodcutter. He lived in a little cottage by a forest.

Every day, the woodcutter went into the forest. He chopped down trees with his sharp, steel ax. Then he sold the wood to the people in town.

The poor woodcutter worked hard. And he was happy. He had his ax. He was able to earn money and buy food for his family.

Underline the character and the setting. The setting has been underlined for you.

Circle the sentences that tell why the woodcutter is happy.

What is the problem at the beginning of the story? Underline the words that tell you.

How does the woodcutter respond to kicking his ax into the water? Circle the words that tell you.

One day, the woodcutter chopped down a tall tree near the river. He stopped to rest. He wanted some water to refresh himself. He put down his ax and reached into the river. But by mistake, he kicked his ax into the water.

"How careless of me!" the woodcutter cried. "My ax is gone! How will I feed my family?"

The woodcutter peered into the river. He looked and looked. But he was unable to see his ax.

The woodcutter sat down, feeling hopeless. Suddenly, a wood fairy appeared. "Why are you sad?" she asked.

The woodcutter told her about his ax.

"Wait," said the fairy. She dove into the river. Soon she **reappeared** with a silver ax.

"This must be your ax," she said.

What fine things the woodcutter could buy with the silver from that ax! He would not need his old ax anymore.

But the silver ax wasn't his. The woodcutter shook his head. "No, that is not my ax," he replied.

How do you know that this is the middle of the story? Why is this part not the end of the story?

How does the woodcutter respond to the fairy's help? Why doesn't he take the silver ax?

What does the woodcutter do each time the fairy comes back with a new ax?

The fairy smiled. She took the silver ax and dove into the river again. Soon she returned with a golden ax. "This must be your ax," the fairy said.

"No, it is not mine," the woodcutter said. "That one is made of gold. It is worth much more than my ax. But I cannot keep it."

The fairy smiled. She took the golden ax and dove into the river again.

Moments later, the helpful fairy reappeared. She held the woodcutter's steel ax.

"That is my ax!" the woodcutter cried.

The fairy handed the ax to him. Then she dove one more time. When she reappeared, she held the silver ax and the gold ax. "These are yours as well," she said. "They are gifts from the river because you have told the truth."

That night, the honest woodcutter returned home. He took all three axes. The gold and silver axes were beautiful. He was happy to have them. But the steel ax was his favorite.

"Honesty is the best reward," he said to himself.

Why do you think the woodcutter likes the steel ax more than the others? Which details in the story help you know?

Check off after each reading.

1st Reading

2nd Reading

3rd Reading

Comprehension Check

1. Retell the details of the beginning of the story.

2. What is the moral of this fable? Explain it in your own words.

3. Read this sentence from the story.

Soon she reappeared with a silver ax.

Circle the prefix in the underlined word. Then write the meaning of the word.

Name: ______________________________

Han-shin and the Bowl of Rice

1 1st Reading Character's Response

What Happens	How Characters Respond
Page 40: Han-shin's family is poor and hungry.	Han-shin . . .
Page 41: The old woman thinks Han-shin looks hungry and gives him a bowl of rice.	Han-shin . . .
Page 42: The old woman gives Han-shin a bowl of rice every day.	Han-shin . . .
Pages 43–44: Han-shin gives the old woman a bowl of gold.	The old woman . . . Then Han-shin . . . The old woman . . .

Name: ____

Han-shin and the Bowl of Rice

2 2nd Reading Central Message

Page 41: What happens at the river? ______________________

____.

These events are important because ______________________

____.

Page 43: Now that Han-shin is grown up, ______________________

____.

Page 44: We know that Han-shin has learned this lesson because

____

____.

3 3rd Reading Critical Thinking

Page 41: The old woman feels that ______________________

____.

Page 44: The old woman stays at the palace because ______________

____.

Name: ______________________________

Not So Clever Fox

1 1st Reading Story Structure

Beginning

Page 50: Fox and Hedgehog are going

Fox wants to

Page 51: The problem is that

Middle

Page 52: Hedgehog

Fox's problem is that

Page 53: Fox asks Hedgehog to

Hedgehog tells Fox to

Ending

Page 54: When the farmer comes, Fox

The farmer

Name: ______________________________

Not So Clever Fox

2 2nd Reading Retell Stories

Page 51: In the beginning, ______________________________

______________________________.

Page 53: In the middle, ______________________________

______________________________.

Page 54: At the end, ______________________________

______________________________.

3 3rd Reading Critical Thinking

Page 51: Hedgehog says this because ______________________________

____

______________________________.

Page 54: I think Fox will be ______________________________

____

______________________________.

Lesson 3

Folktales

A **folktale** is a story that has been told and retold for a long time. In this lesson, you will read three different tellings of one well-known folktale.

Skills Focus

- Point of View
- Compound Words
- Illustrations
- Character's Response
- Root Words
- Compare and Contrast

Point of View

A **point of view** is how a person thinks and feels about something or someone. In a story, each character has a point of view about the other characters and the events in the story.

Let's Try It Read this story.

Ling was tired of the rain. The yard was all muddy. He could not go outside. "I'm bored," he said to his mom.

Ling's mom had an idea. "Let's make berry ice cream," she said.

Ling smiled. He was happy to have something to do. He helped his mom.

Later, the whole family had ice cream. They ate every last bit of it. It was very tasty!

What is Ling's point of view about the rain? Underline the text that tells you. Double underline the family's point of view about berry ice cream.

Discuss How does Ling's point of view change during the story? Why does it change?

Compound Words

A **compound word** is a word that is made up of two smaller words.

Let's Try It

Read the two words in **bold print**.

Put the words together. What is the meaning of the new word?

Words	New Word	Meaning
bed + **time**	bedtime	time for bed
sun + **burn**	sunburn	a burn from the sun

Practice

Read each sentence below. Circle each compound word you find. Write the meaning of each compound word.

1. María will go to the museum this afternoon.

2. We will wait until we see daylight to start our trip.

Read for a Purpose

1. 1st Reading
2. 2nd Reading
3. 3rd Reading

Read along with your teacher. Each time, read for a different purpose. Use the Tools on pages 97 and 98 as you read.

Stone Soup

based on a French folktale

What is the villagers' point of view about soldiers? Underline the text that tells you.

What details in the illustration support the events in the text?

Many years ago, a traveling soldier walked down a long road. He was very hungry and wanted something to eat.

Near **sundown,** the soldier came to a village. "Maybe the villagers will give me some food," he thought.

A young boy saw the soldier coming and told the other villagers.

"Soldiers always want food," said the villagers. "We don't have enough food for ourselves!"

The villagers ran and quickly hid all their food.

When the soldier got to the town square, he greeted the villagers. They had returned to the square. They were warming themselves by a big **outdoor** fire.

"I'm very hungry," the soldier said. "Can you share some food with an old soldier?"

"We're sorry," said the villagers. "We don't have any food!"

The soldier thought that the villagers might be trying to fool him, but he had a trick of his own.

"I'm sorry. You must be hungry, too!" the soldier said. "I could make us all stone soup. That will fill all our bellies!"

What is the soldier's point of view about the villagers? Underline the text that tells you.

How does the cat feel about the soldier? What clues tell you this?

What is the villagers' point of view about making stone soup? Underline the text that helps you know.

Why is the stone in the soup important?

"Soup? Soup from a stone?" the villagers asked. "That's silly! You can't do that."

"You'll see!" said the soldier. "It's easy and delicious! First, I need a big pot."

"I have a big pot!" said one woman. She ran to get it from her house.

"Now I need water," the soldier said.

"We can get water," said two men. They ran to the well and filled up some buckets. They poured the water into the pot.

The soldier reached down and picked up a large stone. He dropped it into the pot with a splash.

Before long, steam rose from the pot. The soldier tasted the soup. "Delicious!" he said. "But it would taste better with some peas and carrots."

"I have some peas and carrots!" said an old man. He ran to get them from his house.

The soldier plopped the peas and carrots into the pot. He tasted the soup again. "Delicious!" he said. "But it would taste even better with beets and potatoes."

"I have some beets and potatoes," said a woman. She brought them from her house.

The villagers are less worried about the soldier. What clues in the illustration show this?

What is the point of view of the soldier and of the villagers now?

Why does the soldier's trick work?

The soldier plopped the beets and potatoes into the pot. He tasted the soup again. "Delicious! But some meat would make this stone soup perfect," he said.

"We have some beef!" said two sisters. They ran to get it from their house.

The soldier dropped the beef into the soup. He stirred the soup. **Everyone** waited. He stirred the soup some more. Finally, he tasted it one last time. "It's ready!" he said.

The soldier filled the bowls up to the top. They all had a wonderful feast in the **moonlight**.

The soldier was happy because his belly was full. The villagers were happy because they learned to make soup from a stone!

Check off after each reading. 1st Reading 2nd Reading 3rd Reading

Illustrations

Illustrations are pictures that you see in a story. Illustrations help you understand the events and characters in a story.

Let's Try It Look at the illustration.

Circle the characters. Put an "X" on details that tell you about the setting.

Discuss Where are the characters? What are the characters doing and feeling?

Comprehension Check

1. How is the villagers' point of view about soldiers different at the end?

2. Which details in the illustrations are never in the text?

3. Read this sentence from the story.

   They all had a wonderful feast in the moonlight.

   Circle the compound word in the sentence. Write the meaning of the compound word.

Respond to Text: Judge

Should the soldier have tricked the villagers into giving him their food? Use details from the story to decide.

Let's Try It List what the soldier and the villagers say and do. List what happens because of the trick, too.

People and Events	Details
The soldier . . .	
The villagers . . .	
The trick . . .	

On Your Own

Do you think the soldier should have tricked the villagers or not? Write a short paragraph that tells your opinion. Support your answer with details from this page and from your Tools on pages 97–98.

Character's Response

A **character** is a person or an animal in a story. We know how characters **respond** to story events by reading what they do, say, think, and feel.

Let's Try It Read this story.

"Emma, the cookout starts at noon," said Mom. "You may come with us if your room is clean."

Emma looked around her room. It was a mess. She heard a knock on the door. "I will help you!" said Carlos. "We can clean fast."

Emma and Carlos cleaned. Then they went to the cookout together.

Underline how Emma responds to her mom. Double underline how Carlos responds to Emma's problem.

Discuss What do Emma and Carlos do to solve Emma's problem?

Root Words

If you do not know the meaning of a long word, you may be able to use its root word to figure out the meaning.

Let's Try It Read this sentence.

The singer smiled when everyone clapped for her.

Look at the underlined word. The root word of the underlined word is *sing*. What does the word *sing* mean? Use the meaning of *sing* to figure out what the word *singer* means in the sentence.

Practice

Read each sentence below. Look at the underlined word. Write the root word and think about its meaning. Then write the meaning of the underlined word.

1. Jonah went out to meet his visitor.

2. Kaylee quickly read her library book and then left.

Read for a Purpose

1 1st Reading

2 2nd Reading

3 3rd Reading

Read along with your teacher. Each time, read for a different purpose. Use the Tools on pages 99 and 100 as you read.

Pebble Tacos

based on the folktale Stone Soup

Underline the text that tells how the traveler responds to seeing the town.

How is the young girl's response to the traveler different from the townspeople's response?

A poor **traveler** rode through the desert on her way home from a long journey. She was hungry and thirsty, but she had no food or water.

Near lunchtime, she saw a little town ahead on the trail. "I'll stop at that town," she thought. "Surely the people there are kind and will give a poor traveler something to eat."

The traveler arrived at the plaza in the center of town. But the townspeople hid in their houses. Only one young girl was outside, sitting on a bale of hay.

"Where is everyone?" the traveler asked. "Is it a holiday?"

"No. People in my town are shy. They always hide when someone new arrives. People here are afraid of **strangers**," the girl said.

"They don't need to be afraid of me," said the traveler. "I am very **helpful**. I want to make pebble tacos for everyone!"

"Pebble tacos?" asked the girl. "What are those?"

"I'll show you," the traveler said. "Please get me some tortillas."

What is different about how the townspeople and the traveler respond to each other?

Why does the girl talk with the traveler?

Underline what the girl asks the townspeople to get for the pebble tacos. Double underline how the townspeople respond.

The girl went to tell the townspeople about the **visitor**. She ran from house to house.

"We have a visitor!" she explained. "She is very nice. She's going to make pebble tacos for all of us!"

"Pebble tacos?" they all said. "What are those?"

"You'll find out," the girl said. "Who has some tortillas?"

Now the people were curious. They had never heard of pebble tacos. Maybe the visitor was nice.

So they gave the girl the tortillas. Then they followed her to the plaza.

At the plaza, the traveler had gathered a pail full of pebbles. The girl gave her the tortillas.

"Great! I'm ready to add the pebbles," the traveler said. "But pebble tacos are always **tasty** with beans. Who has beans?"

None of the people said anything.

"Angel, you have beans!" said the girl with a smile. "I saw you cleaning them this morning!"

"That's right. I'll get them," said Angel. He went to his home. He came back with a pot of beans.

Underline how the townspeople respond when the traveler asks for beans. Double underline what Angel does after the girl talks to him.

Underline the text that tells how the traveler responds when it is time to add the pebbles.

What is the same about what Ana and Sofía do? What is different?

What is the real reason the traveler does not add the pebbles to the tacos?

The traveler added the beans. "I'm ready to add the pebbles," she said. "But pebble tacos are always tasty with tomatoes. And cheese! Who has some?"

No one said anything.

"Ana, you have tomatoes in your garden!" said the girl. "And Sofía, you made cheese just yesterday."

"Okay, we'll get them," said Ana and Sofía. They ran to their houses. They came back with tomatoes and cheese.

The traveler added the tomatoes and cheese.

It was time to add the pebbles. But wait! "Now there's no room for the pebbles," the traveler cried. "We'll have to eat the tacos just the way they are!"

The pebble tacos were the best tacos they had ever eaten. Everyone ate until they were stuffed like tacos!

Check off after each reading.

1st Reading 2nd Reading 3rd Reading

Compare and Contrast

When you **compare** two things, you look at how they are the same. When you **contrast** two things, you look at how they are different.

Let's Try It Read this story.

Caleb and Sara were planning a party. "I like to help Dad cook," said Sara. "I will plan the food."

"I like to play games," said Caleb. "I will plan the games we will play."

"We'll need someone to decorate, too," said Dad.

"I love balloons!" cried Caleb.

"I love balloons, too!" smiled Sara. "Let's blow up some together."

Underline the text that tells what Sara likes. Double underline the text that tells what Caleb likes. Circle the text that tells what Caleb and Sara both like.

Discuss What do Sara, Caleb, and Dad each plan and help with for the party?

Comprehension Check

1. How do the girl and all the townspeople respond when they hear about pebble tacos?

2. Compare and contrast how the traveler feels at the beginning and at the end of the story.

3. Read this sentence from the story.

   She was hungry and thirsty, but she had no food or water.

   Write the root word of the underlined word. Then write the meaning of the underlined word.

Respond to Text: Compare and Contrast

What are the central messages, or lessons, in "Stone Soup" and "Pebble Tacos"? Are the messages the same or different?

Let's Try It List your ideas about each story in the chart. Circle the ideas that are the same for both folktales.

Central Messages in "Stone Soup"	Central Messages in "Pebble Tacos"

On Your Own

Write a paragraph that compares the central messages in each story. How are the messages the same? Support your answer with details from this page and from your Tools on pages 97–100.

Take-Home Book

1. Remove this folktale from your book.

2. Read it three times. Use what you have learned about folktales.

   1 1st Reading — Point of View

   2 2nd Reading — Compare and Contrast

   3 3rd Reading — Critical Thinking

3. Answer the questions in the Comprehension Check on page 96.

Name: ____________________

Read for a Purpose

1 1st Reading
Point of View

2 2nd Reading
Compare and Contrast

3 3rd Reading
Critical Thinking

Read the text three times. Use the skills you have learned. Then complete the Comprehension Check.

Penny Stew

based on the folktale Stone Soup

It was the holiday weekend. The neighborhood was having its big party. Everyone on the block was there.

People always had fun. There was music. There were games. There was a clown. There was face painting.

The best part was dinner. Every cook on the block brought a special dish. The neighbors couldn't wait to taste them all. They were ready to eat!

What is each cook's point of view about whose party food is the best?

But the cooks always argued about whose food was the best.

Jay Jones said, "My Seafood Surprise always wins a prize!"

Eva Sanchez said, "Folks can't stop lickin' their fingers when they eat my Crispy Chicken!"

"You're both wrong!" said Simon Price. "My Veggie Rice makes folks eat twice!"

The cooks shouted back and forth. It was very loud!

Suddenly, tiny Sally yelled, "Hush!"

The cooks all stopped shouting.

"I'm making Penny Stew!" said Sally. "And here's what I need you to do. Please BE QUIET!"

"Penny Stew?" the cooks all asked. "What's that?"

"It's easy," said Sally. "I drop a penny in a pot. A sizzling fire makes it hot. Before you count to 102, we'll all be eating tasty stew!"

Sally's mom put a big pot of water on the fire. Sally dropped in the penny. Plop!

What is Sally's point of view about all the shouting? Underline the text that tells you.

What is the same about what Jay and Eva do for Sally? What is different?

"That's it?" asked the cooks.

"You'll see," Sally explained. "But you know what? Some tasty shrimp and fish would make this a special dish."

"I have seafood," said Jay Jones. "Here's some fish and shrimp."

Sally added them to the stew.

"You know what?" said Sally. "Some meat would make this good to eat."

"Here's some chicken," said Eva Sanchez.

Sally added it to the stew, too.

"You know what?" said Sally. "Some vegetables and rice would be really nice."

"Here's some Veggie Rice!" said Simon Price.

The stew bubbled and steamed. The smells tickled the neighbors' noses. Mouths started to water.

"It's ready!" said Sally. Everyone got a big bowl of stew.

"This is the best dish by far!" shouted the cooks.

Sally **sweetly** smiled. "See what we can do, when we *all* make Penny Stew!"

How is Penny Stew the same as the three other dishes? How is it different?

What lesson do the three cooks learn in this story? How can you use this lesson in your own life?

Check off after each reading. 1st Reading 2nd Reading 3rd Reading

Comprehension Check

1. What do the three cooks *always* do at the block party? Write one thing they always do for the party. Then name one way they always respond to each other.

2. How does the illustration on page 95 show everyone's point of view about Penny Stew?

3. Read this sentence from the story.

   Sally sweetly smiled.

   Write the root word of the underlined word. Then write the meaning of the underlined word.

Name: ______________________________

Stone Soup

1 1st Reading Point of View

Characters	Point of View
Page 72: What is the villagers' point of view about soldiers?	
Page 73: What is the soldier's point of view about the villagers?	
Page 74: What is the villagers' point of view about stone soup?	
Page 76: What is the point of view of the soldier and of the villagers at the end?	

Name: ____

Stone Soup

2 2nd Reading Illustrations

Page 72: Some details in the illustration that support the text are

____

____.

Page 73: The cat ____________ the soldier. The clues that tell me are

____

____.

Page 75: The villagers ____

____.

3 3rd Reading Critical Thinking

Page 74: The stone is important because ______________________

____.

Page 76: The soldier's trick works because ______________________

____

____.

Name: ______________________________

Pebble Tacos

1 1st Reading Character's Response

What Happens	How Characters Respond
Page 82: The traveler sees a town.	The traveler . . .
Page 84: The girl tells the townspeople that the visitor will make pebble tacos.	The girl . . . The townspeople . . .
Page 85: The traveler asks for beans. The girl tells Angel she saw him cleaning beans.	The townspeople . . . Angel . . .
Page 86: It is time to add the pebbles to the tacos.	The traveler . . .

Name: ______________________________

Pebble Tacos

2 2nd Reading Compare and Contrast

Page 82: The way that the young girl's response is different is that ____

____

______________________________.

Page 83: The townspeople ______________________________

______________________________.

The traveler is different because ______________________________

______________________________.

Page 86: Ana and Sofía both ______________________________

______________________________.

Ana ______________________________. Sofía ______________________________.

3 3rd Reading Critical Thinking

Page 83: The girl talks to the traveler because ______________________________

______________________________.

Page 86: The traveler doesn't add the pebbles because ______________________________

______________________________.

Lesson 4

Poetry

Poets create **poetry** by using carefully chosen words to show ideas or feelings. A poem can paint a picture in your mind or tell you a story. In this lesson, you will read several poems that help you see the world in a new way.

Skills Focus

- Inferences
- Real-Life Connections
- Central Message
- Ask and Answer Questions
- Shades of Meaning
- Rhythm and Meaning

Inferences

An **inference** is a good guess you make about something that an author does not tell you. You can make inferences about the setting, characters, feelings, or events in a text.

Let's Try It Read this paragraph.

Matt and Juan were swimming.
Juan's dad called them for lunch.
After lunch, they built a sand castle.
Then they went swimming again.
It was fun.

Underline clues that tell you where Matt and Juan are.

Discuss Where are Matt and Juan? Support your ideas with clues from the text.

Real-Life Connections

When you make a connection between a word and the world, you are identifying a **real-life connection**. You can connect words you know with your own experiences.

Let's Try It Read this poem. Connect a few words to your life.

Day to Night

I look up in the daylight,
Up into the sky.
I see almost a shape,
A broken circle way up high.

What, I wonder, can it be?
I know that I should know!
It's the moon, oh silly me,
Showing off its glow.

Practice

Give an example of each underlined word in the poem. Write what the underlined word might be like.

1. shape: ______________________________

   Description: ______________________________

2. silly: ______________________________

   Description: ______________________________

1 1st Reading

2 2nd Reading

3 3rd Reading

Read along with your teacher. Each time, read for a different purpose. Use the Tools on pages 123 and 124 as you read.

Keep a Poem in Your Pocket

by Beatrice Schenk de Regniers

Keep a poem in your pocket
and a **picture** in your head
and you'll never feel **lonely**
at night when you're in bed.

What is the speaker of the poem asking you to do? Circle the words that tell you. Why does the speaker of the poem want you to do this?

The little poem will **sing** to you
the little picture bring to you
a dozen **dreams** to **dance** to you
at night when you're in bed.

So —
Keep a picture in your pocket
and a poem in your head
and you'll never feel lonely
at night when you're in bed.

What does the speaker of the poem want you to know about poems and dreams? Underline clues that tell you.

What is the central message of this poem?

Would this poem be a good one to keep in your head at night? Why or why not?

What is the secret in this poem? Underline clues that help you know.

What is the central message of this poem? Circle clues that help you know.

Does the speaker of the poem do a good job of keeping the secret? Why do you think this?

We Have a Secret

Anonymous

We have a **secret**, just we three,
The robin and I and the sweet cherry tree;
The bird told the tree and the tree told me,
And nobody knows it but just we three.
But of course the robin knows it best,
Because she built the — I shan't tell the rest;
And laid the four little — **somethings** — in it —
I am afraid I shall tell it every minute.
But if the tree and the robin don't **peep**,
I'll try my best the secret to keep;
Though I know when the little birds fly about,
Then the whole secret will be out.

Check off after each reading.

1st Reading 2nd Reading 3rd Reading

Central Message

The **central message** in a poem is the main idea, image, or feeling that the poet shares with you. It is what the poet most wants you to understand.

Let's Try It Reread this poem.

Day to Night

I look up in the daylight,
Up into the sky.
I see almost a shape,
A broken circle way up high.

What, I wonder, can it be?
I know that I should know!
It's the moon, oh silly me,
Showing off its glow.

Circle words that help you understand the message of the poem.

Discuss What do you think is the message of this poem? Share your ideas with a partner. Use the words you circled as you talk.

Comprehension Check

1. In the poem "We Have a Secret," what has to happen before "the little birds fly about"?

2. In the poem "Keep a Poem in Your Pocket," what does the speaker mean by "Keep a poem in your pocket . . . and you'll never feel lonely"?

3. Name a time when you might be lonely. Then write how you feel when you are lonely.

Respond to Text: Analyze

Think about the poems "Keep a Poem in Your Pocket" and "We Have a Secret." Imagine that the speaker of each poem is your friend telling you something. How does the speaker of each poem tell you his or her ideas?

Let's Try It List words and phrases that show how the speaker of each poem talks to you.

"Keep a Poem in Your Pocket"	"We Have a Secret"
talks directly to me	tells me about the secret

On Your Own

Which poem feels more connected to you and your life? Write a short paragraph that analyzes how each speaker connects to you. Which connection feels stronger? Use words from the poems and what you wrote on this page to support your answer with details.

Ask and Answer Questions

You can ask **questions** about a poem before, during, and after you read it. Then you can look for **answers** in the poem.

Let's Try It Read this poem.

A Friendly Ride

Kim took a ride on a bus one day.
She made a new friend along the way.
Her new friend was kind,
Kim was happy to find;
And together they said, "Can we stay?"

Who is this poem about? Underline the words that tell you the answer. Where does the poem take place? Double underline the words that tell you.

Discuss How do Kim and her new friend feel at the end of the poem? How do you know?

Shades of Meaning

Words like *hop, skip,* and *jump* tell about actions that are like each other but different in small ways. These small differences in meaning are called **shades of meaning**.

Let's Try It Read this poem. Talk about the actions in it.

Let's Move!

I like to walk and hike and tramp.
You like to stomp and clomp and stamp.
We like to move and sway and wriggle.
So many ways to laugh and giggle!

Practice

Read each word. Then write the words in order, from weakest to strongest, in the chart.

1. whisper yell talk

whisper		

2. giggle grin laugh

Read for a Purpose

1 1st Reading

2 2nd Reading

3 3rd Reading

Read along with your teacher. Each time, read for a different purpose. Use the Tools on pages 125 and 126 as you read.

Kite

Anonymous

A kite on the ground
Is just paper and string . . .
But up in the air—
It will dance and sing.

What is this poem about? Underline the answer. Where does a kite dance and sing? Double underline the answer.

A kite in the air
Will **dance** and will **caper** . . .
But back on the ground —
Is just string and paper.

What is the kite made of? Underline the answer.

Circle the words that rhyme in the poem. How do these words create rhythm?

How does the kite change in the poem?

What is the poem about? Underline the words that tell you when to jump.

Which words create rhythm in the poem? Explain why.

How are the last four lines like the first line? How are they different?

Rope Rhyme

by Eloise Greenfield

Get set, ready now, **jump** right in
Bounce and kick and giggle and spin
Listen to the rope when it hits the ground
Listen to that clappedy-slappedy sound
Jump right up when it tells you to
Come back down, whatever you do
Count to a hundred, count by ten
Start to count all over again
That's what jumping is all about
Get set, ready now,
jump
right
out!

Check off after each reading.

1st Reading   2nd Reading   3rd Reading

Rhythm and Meaning

Many poems have a **rhythm**, or beat, like a song. A poet may use rhythm in a poem to emphasize certain words and create meaning.

Let's Try It Reread this poem.

Let's Move!

I like to walk and hike and tramp.
You like to stomp and clomp and stamp.
We like to move and sway and wriggle.
So many ways to laugh and giggle!

Circle four pairs of words that rhyme in the poem. Underline two words that begin with the same two sounds. What phrases in the first three lines have a repeated word? Double underline those phrases.

Discuss What repeated patterns in the poem help to create rhythm? How do these patterns help you better understand the poem?

Comprehension Check

1. Why does the speaker of the poem "Rope Rhyme" tell the jumper to *listen, jump,* and *count*?

2. List some important words that are repeated in "Kite." How do these repeated words help you understand what the kite is doing in the poem?

   Words:

   These repeated words help me understand that

3. Think about the word *spin* in "Rope Rhyme." What is a word that is like *spin* but stronger? What is a word that is weaker? Write the words in order from weakest to strongest.

	spin	

Respond to Text: Compare and Contrast

The poets who wrote "Keep a Poem in Your Pocket" and "Kite" both made nonliving things seem alive. One poet makes a poem seem alive. The other poet makes a kite seem alive. Compare and contrast how each poem does this.

Let's Try It The poets make a poem and a kite seem alive. List your ideas about how they do this. Circle ideas that are the same.

"Keep a Poem in Your Pocket"	"Kite"
makes a poem seem alive	makes a kite seem alive

On Your Own

Write a paragraph that compares and contrasts how each poet makes a nonliving thing seem alive. Which poem does this better? Support your answer with details. Use what you wrote on this page and in your Tools on pages 123–126.

Take-Home Book

1. Remove these poems from your book.

2. Read the poems three times. Use what you have learned about poetry.

   1 1st Reading — Ask and Answer Questions

   2 2nd Reading — Rhythm and Meaning

   3 3rd Reading — Critical Thinking

3. Answer the questions in the Comprehension Check on page 122.

Name: ______________________________

Read for a Purpose

Read the text three times. Use the skills you have learned. Then complete the Comprehension Check.

1 1st Reading
Ask and Answer Questions

2 2nd Reading
Rhythm and Meaning

3 3rd Reading
Critical Thinking

April Rain Song

by Langston Hughes

Let the rain kiss you.
Let the rain beat upon your head with silver liquid drops.
Let the rain sing you a lullaby.

The rain makes still **pools** on the sidewalk.
The rain makes running pools in the gutter.
The rain plays a little sleep-song on our roof at night—

And I love the rain.

What does the speaker of the poem ask you to do?

Circle the repeated phrases in the poem. How do these phrases give the poem rhythm? How do they help you understand the poem?

Read the first four lines aloud. Is the rhythm smooth or uneven? Does it remind you of being on a swing? Why or why not?

The Swing

by Robert Louis Stevenson

How do you like to go up in a swing,
    Up in the air so blue?
Oh, I do think it the pleasantest thing
    Ever a child can do!

Up in the air and over the wall,
Till I can see so wide,
Rivers and trees and cattle and all
Over the countryside —

Till I look down on the garden green,
Down on the roof so brown —
Up in the air I go flying again,
Up in the air and down!

What does the speaker in the poem see? Underline the words that tell you what the speaker "can see so wide."

Both poems tell about enjoying something. Which poem creates a stronger picture in your mind? Why?

Check off after each reading. 1st Reading 2nd Reading 3rd Reading

✓ Comprehension Check

1. Where and how is the speaker of the poem "The Swing" swinging? What words in the poem tell you this?

2. What is the central message of "April Rain Song"?

3. The poet uses the word *pools* in "April Rain Song." Think of a kind of pool and write what it is like.

Name: ______________________________

Keep a Poem in Your Pocket
We Have a Secret

1 1st Reading **Inferences**

Page 105 Clues | **Inference**

Clues	Inference
poems will dreams to	

Page 106 Clues | **Inference**

Clues	Inference
Who? The robin	The robin has built
What? The robin	The robin laid four little
When	The four little

Name: ______________________________

Keep a Poem in Your Pocket
We Have a Secret

2 2nd Reading Central Message

Page 104: The speaker of the poem wants you to ______________

______________________________.

Page 105: The central message is that ______________

______________________________.

Page 106: The central message is that ______________

______________________________.

3 3rd Reading Critical Thinking

Page 105: I think this poem is __________ to keep in my head at night.

I think this because ______________________________

______________________________.

Page 106: I think the speaker ______________ do a good job of keeping the secret. I think this because ______________________________

______________________________.

Name: ____________________

Kite / Rope Rhyme

1 1st Reading **Ask and Answer Questions**

Question	Answer
Page 112: What is the poem about?	
Page 112: Where does a kite dance and sing?	
Page 113: What is a kite made of?	
Page 114: What is the poem about?	
Page 114: How do you know when to jump the rope?	

Name: ____

Kite / Rope Rhyme

2 2nd Reading Rhythm and Meaning

Page 113: The words that rhyme ______________________________

____.

They are important to the meaning because ______________________

____.

Page 114: The words that help me hear the rhythm are ____________

____.

These words help me ______________________________________

____.

3 3rd Reading Critical Thinking

Page 113: The kite changes _________________________________

____.

Page 114: The lines are the same because _______________________

____.

The lines are different because __________________________________

____.

Lesson 5

Social Studies Texts

When you read a **social studies text**, you read information about real people, places, and events. In this lesson, you'll read three social studies texts about caring for nature.

Skills Focus

- Main Topic
- Context Clues
- Images
- Connect Ideas
- Glossaries
- Ask and Answer Questions

✔ Main Topic

A social studies text usually tells about one main topic. A topic can be a subject or idea. The **main topic** is what the text is mostly about.

Let's Try It Read this short article.

Beautiful Denali

Denali National Park is in Alaska. The park has the highest mountain peak in North America. Every year thousands of people visit Denali. They hike, bike, fish, and camp. The park is home to many wild animals.

▲ Mount McKinley is in Denali National Park.

Underline the title. Double underline a sentence that tells what the article is mostly about. That is the main topic.

Discuss What does this paragraph tell you about the main topic?

Context Clues

Context clues help you figure out the meaning of a word you do not know. Context clues may be words in the same sentence as the word you do not know. They can also be words in another sentence nearby.

Let's Try It

Read these sentences.

The law made California **responsible** for protecting Yosemite. It became the state's job to care for the land.

To learn what *responsible* means, reread the second sentence. Underline the context clues for *responsible*.

Practice

Use context clues to figure out the meaning of the words below in **bold print**. Underline the context clues that helped you. Circle the meaning of the word.

1. Land, water, plants, and animals are all **resources**.

   things in nature that people use

   helpful books like dictionaries

2. Each park is a **treasure** for the nation. That's because each park is a very important outdoor area.

   something outside   something very special

Read for a Purpose

1 1st Reading
2 2nd Reading
3 3rd Reading

Read along with your teacher. Each time, read for a different purpose. Use the Tools on pages 155 and 156 as you read.

America's National Parks

▶ Explorers found amazing natural wonders in Yosemite Valley.

Underline the title of the selection. According to the title, what is this selection mostly about?

Natural Wonders

Almost 200 years ago, explorers arrived at a valley in California. Long before that time, Native Americans had lived there. The beauty of the valley **amazed** the visitors. They saw tall mountains. They heard tumbling waterfalls.

Soon, more visitors arrived. Some came to enjoy the natural beauty. But others came to dig for gold. They harmed the land and animals. A visitor named the valley. He called it Yosemite. *Yosemite* was a Native American word. But gold miners drove the Native Americans out of the valley.

Yellowstone National Park

Old Faithful is a geyser in Yellowstone. A geyser is a hot spring that sends hot water up into the air.

The First National Park

Some people wanted to conserve Yosemite. To **conserve** means to care for and protect resources. Land, water, plants, and animals are all **resources**. The people asked the United States government to protect Yosemite. In 1864, a new law made California **responsible** for protecting Yosemite. It became the state's job to care for the land.

The idea of conserving natural places spread. A few years later, the government created the first national park. It is called Yellowstone National Park. Yellowstone is also full of natural wonders. There are canyons and mountains. Rivers sprawl across the land. Hot water shoots out of **geysers**.

What is this page mostly about? Underline the text that helps you figure out the main topic.

Circle the title of the map. Where is Yellowstone National Park?

How does the photograph help you understand what a geyser is?

What is the first paragraph mostly about? Underline a sentence that tells you the main topic.

Was it a good idea for the United States government to create national parks? Why or why not?

Creating More National Parks

How did the government create national parks? The government took control of special outdoor places. It cared for them. Visitors from all over could enjoy the parks. Special rules protected the land. The rules also protected the animals and plants.

After Yellowstone, the government created more national parks. An island in Michigan was the second national park. In 1890, Yosemite Valley became a national park, too.

▼ John Muir was a famous nature author. He helped Yosemite Valley become Yosemite National Park.

◀ The Pinnacles in Pinnacles National Park stick up above the park land below.

Many Special Places

Since 1872, many new parks have opened. Today there are 59 national parks. Each park is its own special place. There are desert parks. There are mountain parks. There are even parks in oceans. Each park is a **treasure** for the nation. That's because each park is a very important outdoor area.

In 2013, Pinnacles National Park became the newest national park. It is in California. The park is named for the unusual rocks there. They are called the Pinnacles.

What is the first paragraph mostly about? Underline the sentence that tells you the main topic.

How does the photograph help you understand what the Pinnacles are?

▶ A ranger helps demonstrate Native American weaving. The National Park Service teaches visitors about Native American culture and history.

What is the main topic of the first paragraph? What does it tell you about America's national parks?

Why is the National Park Service important for America?

The National Park Service

In 1916, the government created the National Park Service to take care of the national parks. It also helps preserve Native American sites in some parks. The National Park Service works with Native American groups who once lived there.

Each year, nearly 300 million people visit America's national parks. They come to breathe fresh air. They watch the wild animals. They climb the beautiful mountains. Thanks to the National Park Service, these special resources are protected for everyone to enjoy.

Check off after each reading. 1st Reading 2nd Reading 3rd Reading

Images

Social studies texts often have images such as **maps** and **photographs**. They give you information in a different way. They can help you better understand the text.

Let's Try It Use the two images to answer the questions.

Denali National Park

▲ An entrance to Denali National Park

Circle the area on the map that shows where Denali National Park is. Draw a box around the image that helps you see what Denali National Park looks like.

Discuss What information does the map key give you?

Comprehension Check

1. Reread page 134. What does the information on this page tell about the main topic of the selection?

2. Look at the map on page 131. Which state is above, or north of, Yellowstone National Park?

3. Read this sentence from the selection.

   Hot water shoots out of geysers.

   Circle the word or words that help you understand the meaning of *geysers*. Then write the meaning of the word.

Respond to Text: Connect

Years ago, people in America wanted to conserve the country's beautiful outdoor spaces. They asked the United States government to help. The government took action. You can connect the events and explain why the solutions were good ideas.

Let's Try It

Read each problem below. How did people and the government solve each problem?

Problem	Solution
1. People were harming places like Yosemite and Yellowstone.	Other people asked . . .
2. The government wanted to conserve these places.	The government . . .

On Your Own

Think about the solutions to the problems. Write a short paragraph that tells why the solutions were good ideas. Support your answer with details. You can use what you wrote on this page and in your Tools on pages 155–156.

✔ Connect Ideas

Connecting ideas means linking one idea with another. You can connect events in the order in which they happen. This order is called the **sequence**.

Let's Try It Read this paragraph.

Dian Fossey was born in California in 1932. When she grew up, she visited Africa. There she saw wild mountain gorillas. Fossey decided to learn all about these animals. A few years later, she started a research center in Africa. Fossey spent years watching mountain gorillas. In 1983, she wrote a famous book about what she learned.

Underline the text that tells what happened when Dian Fossey first went to Africa. Double underline the text that tells when she started her research center.

Discuss What sequence of events led to the famous book that Dian Fossey wrote? What kind of information do you think is in the book she wrote?

Glossaries

A **glossary** is a list of words found at the end of some informational texts. It gives the meanings of some of the difficult words in the text. A glossary helps you learn the meanings of new words.

Let's Try It
Read this part of a glossary.

crops plants that are grown on a farm

decline to become less in number

environment the natural world in a place, including land, water, and plants

Underline the entry that would best help you understand an informational text about what farmers do.

Practice

Read each set of sentences below. Circle the sentence that makes the most sense. Use the glossary above to help you.

1. **A.** The nature writer wanted to save the environment.
   B. Steven went to the environment to buy shoes.
2. **A.** The number of crops declined because there was no rain.
   B. The number of trees declined when more trees were planted.

Read for a Purpose

1 1st Reading

2 2nd Reading

3 3rd Reading

Read along with your teacher. Each time, read for a different purpose. Use the Tools on pages 157 and 158 as you read.

The Tree Mother of Africa

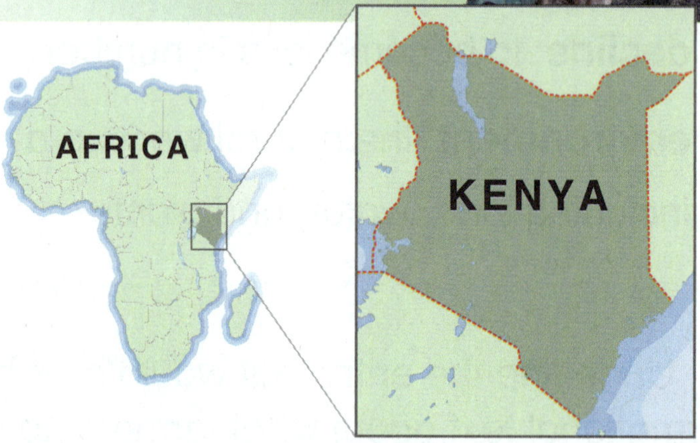

What two things did Wangari Maathai do when she left her village? Underline the text that tells you.

What did Wangari Maathai think was not fair? Circle the sentence that tells you.

Wangari Maathai grew up in a small village in Kenya in Africa. Nearby, thick forests covered the land. In their shade, streams flowed. In sunny fields, farmers grew crops. The land provided food and water for everyone.

As a child, Maathai wanted to become a scientist. But people told her that only boys could grow up to be scientists. Maathai thought this was not fair.

So, when Maathai got older, she left her village. She went to college and became a scientist. After many years, she returned home. But what she saw shocked her.

Maathai saw that the land had changed. First, **timber** companies had cut down trees to get wood. Then farmers had planted **crops** on the cleared land. Everything looked different.

At first, the change seemed good. In Maathai's country, people earned money for cutting timber. They used firewood to cook food. But most of the trees were gone. The changes had started to destroy the **environment**.

Because so many trees were gone, the tree roots were gone, too. Tree roots held soil in place. Without tree roots, rain washed the soil away. Before long, crops would not grow. The amount of food from farms **declined**. There was less and less of it.

Why were tree roots important for crops to grow?

◀ Wangari Maathai was shocked to see large areas of land without trees.

▶ People had to carry water long distances.

What event happened after firewood became scarce? Underline the text that tells you.

How did deforestation cause water to dry up? Circle the text that tells you.

Deforestation, or the loss of trees, also caused water to dry up. The shade of trees kept water cool. Without trees, the water in lakes and streams became warm. The hot sun made the water disappear. The soil became dry. Crops would not grow. Water was **scarce**. It was hard to find water to drink.

Without trees, there was also no firewood. People had to walk to **distant** forests to get wood. They had to walk long distances to get water, too. Life in many African villages became harder.

Even worse, the loss of forests caused people to fight. People fought over the land that still had forests. This worried Wangari Maathai. She wanted to fix these problems.

Wangari Maathai knew Africa could not be peaceful without forests. People needed water, wood, and food. She came up with a solution. Her idea was to plant new trees to make new forests.

In many parts of Africa, women gather firewood and water for their homes. So Maathai thought that women could help. She asked them to plant new trees. The women earned a small amount of money for every tree they planted.

Maathai called her project the Green Belt Movement. Its goal was to plant a belt, or band, of new green trees across Africa.

Maathai discovered problems caused by deforestation. What was her idea to solve the problems? Underline the text that tells you.

Why did Maathai think women would want to help plant trees? Circle a sentence that tells you.

▼ African women in the Green Belt Movement planted new trees.

▶ In 2004, Wangari Maathai won the Nobel Peace Prize. Each year the prize is given to a person who helps the world become more peaceful.

▲ A young tree is ready to be planted.

Underline a detail that tells how many trees people in the Green Belt Movement had planted as of 2011. What are community groups doing today?

Women across Africa began to plant trees. As the trees grew, the roots spread. They held more soil in place. They shaded more ground. This helped the soil become moist. It held more water.

Across Africa, forests started to return. The soil became good for farming again. Thanks to hardworking women, a wasteland was restored.

As of 2011, African women had planted more than 30 million trees. Today there are more than 4,000 community groups in the Green Belt Movement. These groups follow the dream of Wangari Maathai, the Tree Mother of Africa.

Why is Tree Mother of Africa a good nickname for Wangari Maathai?

Check off after each reading. 1st Reading 2nd Reading 3rd Reading

Ask and Answer Questions

You can ask **questions** about the topic in an informational text. Then you can look for the **answers** in the text.

Let's Try It

Read this paragraph.

Marjory Stoneman Douglas spent most of her life working to save the Everglades. The Everglades is a large wilderness area in Florida. In 1915, Douglas moved to Florida. She fell in love with the Everglades. She wrote about its beauty. She helped convince the government to make the Everglades a national park.

▲ The Florida Everglades

Who is this paragraph about? Underline the text that tells you. Where did this person live? Double underline the text that tells you.

Discuss What questions do you have about Marjory Stoneman Douglas?

Comprehension Check

1. Why did Wangari Maathai start the Green Belt Movement?

2. What do the people of the Green Belt Movement do today?

3. Read these two entries from a glossary. Write the word in **bold print** that best completes the sentence.

decline to become less in number

restore to fix something so it is the way it used to be

The Green Belt Movement helped to __________ the forests in Africa by planting trees.

Respond to Text: Compare and Contrast

"America's National Parks" and "The Tree Mother of Africa" both tell about people helping to save natural places.

Let's Try It What do the texts tell you about saving the environment? How are the details in the texts alike? How are they different?

"America's National Parks"	Both	"The Tree Mother of Africa"

On Your Own

Write a short paragraph that tells how real people did different and similar things to help the environment in "America's National Parks" and "The Tree Mother of Africa." Support your answer with details. You can use what you wrote on this page and in your Tools on pages 155–158.

Take-Home Book

1. Remove this social studies text from your book.

2. Read it three times. Use what you have learned about social studies texts.

   1 1st Reading **Main Topic**

   2 2nd Reading **Connect Ideas**

   3 3rd Reading **Critical Thinking**

3. Answer the questions in the **Comprehension Check** on page 154.

Name: ______________________________

Read for a Purpose

1 1st Reading
Main Topic

2 2nd Reading
Connect Ideas

3 3rd Reading
Critical Thinking

Read the text three times. Use the skills you have learned. Then complete the Comprehension Check.

The Story of Arbor Day

People around the world enjoy holidays. Some holidays honor people. Some celebrate events in history. The Fourth of July is a holiday like that.

One holiday honors trees. It is called Arbor Day. *Arbor* is a word from the Latin language. It means "tree." Every year, people in many countries celebrate Arbor Day. On Arbor Day, people plant trees.

What is this selection mostly about? Underline the text that tells the main topic. This text is already underlined for you.

What event happened when J. Sterling Morton was a young man? Double underline the text that tells you.

Arbor Day began in 1872. It was the idea of a man named J. Sterling Morton.

Morton grew up in Michigan. When he was a young man, he moved to Nebraska. Nebraska is in the middle of the country. In the late 1800s, many Americans moved there. There was good farmland on the **prairie**. The large, flat grassland had good soil. Because of the soil, crops grew well.

▶ J. Sterling Morton

▶ J. Sterling Morton moved from Detroit to Nebraska City.

◀ In Michigan (left), there had been many trees. But the prairie (below) was flat, with few trees.▼

Morton was not a farmer. But he liked to write about farming. In Nebraska City, he started a newspaper. He wrote about agriculture.

One thing bothered Morton. He saw that there were not many trees on the prairie. In Michigan, there were lots of trees. As a boy, he had loved the forests. But the prairie was different. On the flat plains, hardly any trees grew. Morton thought this was a problem.

What did Morton do after he moved to Nebraska City? Double underline the sentence that tells you.

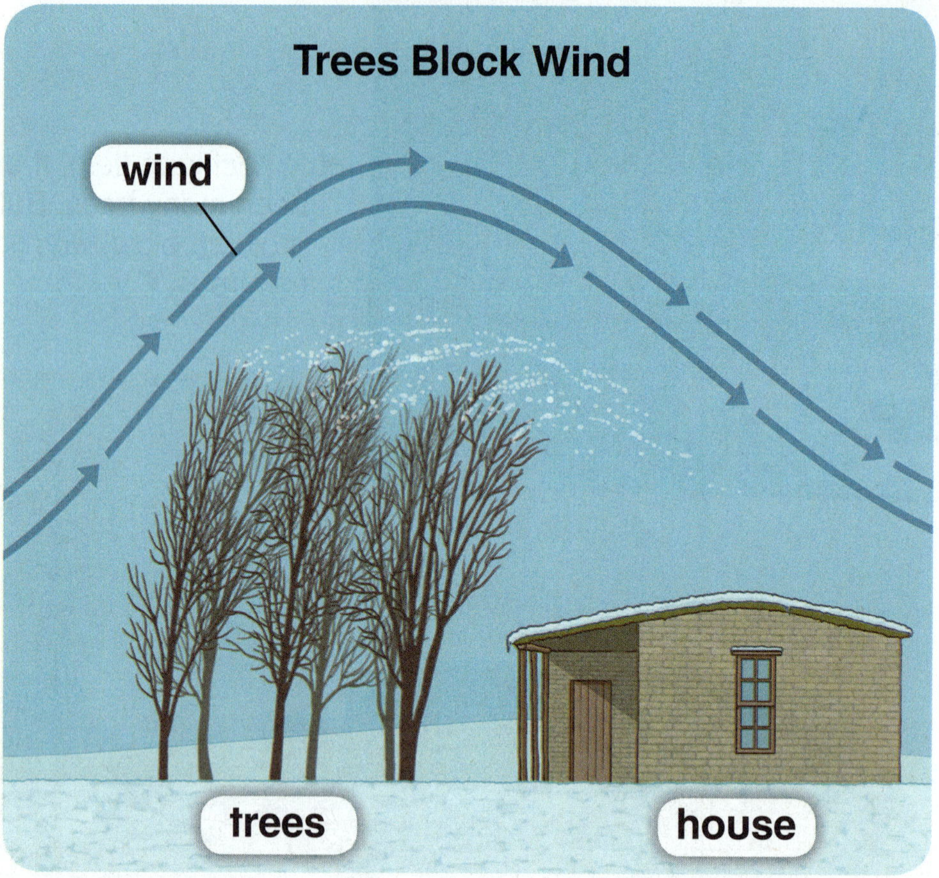

▲ On the prairie, cold winds often made homes very cold. Trees could block the wind and protect people's homes.

What is this page mostly about? Underline the sentence that tells you.

Morton felt that Nebraska needed more trees. He wrote articles in his newspaper. He said that people should plant trees.

Morton pointed out why trees were important. The roots of trees held soil in place. Without trees, the soil could wash away. Trees could also give shade in the hot summers. They could block cold prairie winds in winter. Trees gave people wood for fires. People could use wood from trees to build houses.

Today, people in Nebraska and all over the world plant trees to celebrate Arbor Day.

Morton decided to create a special holiday. He called it Arbor Day. On Arbor Day, people would plant trees. Morton wanted Nebraska to have many trees.

People in Nebraska liked the idea. So, in 1872, Arbor Day was born. There were prizes for people who planted the most trees. Nebraskans planted more than one million trees.

Soon other states began celebrating Arbor Day. Today, all 50 states celebrate this holiday. It is usually in April. Arbor Day spread to many other countries, too. All around the world, people plant trees. Thanks to J. Sterling Morton, the world is a greener place.

When did Arbor Day start in Nebraska? Double underline the text that tells you. What events happened after that?

Why is the world a greener place thanks to J. Sterling Morton?

Check off after each reading.

1st Reading 2nd Reading 3rd Reading

Comprehension Check

1. How did J. Sterling Morton tell people about his idea for Arbor Day?

2. Look at the map on page 150. Where did J. Sterling Morton live before he moved to Nebraska?

3. Read these sentences from the selection.

   There was good farmland on the prairie.
   The large, flat grasslands had good soil.

   Circle the word or words that help you understand the meaning of *prairie*. Then write the meaning.

Name: ______________________________

America's National Parks

1 1st Reading Main Topic

Page 130
The selection is mostly about . . .

Page 131
This page is mostly about . . .

Page 132
The first paragraph is mostly about . . .

Page 133
The first paragraph is mostly about . . .

Page 134
The first paragraph is mostly about . . .

This topic tells me . . .

Name: ______________________________

America's National Parks

2 2nd Reading Images

Page 131: The map shows me that Yellowstone is

______________________________.

Page 131: The photograph shows me that a geyser

______________________________.

Page 133: The photograph shows me that the Pinnacles

____

______________________________.

3 3rd Reading Critical Thinking

Page 132: It was a ____________________ idea to create the national parks because ______________________________

______________________________.

Page 134: The National Park Service is important for America because

____

______________________________.

Name: ______________________________

The Tree Mother of Africa

1 1st Reading **Connect Ideas**

Page 140: When Wangari Maathai left her village, she . . .

Event:

Page 142: After firewood became scarce, people . . .

Event:

Page 143: Maathai's idea to solve the problems was . . .

Event:

Page 144: Today, Green Belt Movement community groups continue to . . .

Event:

Name: ______________________________

The Tree Mother of Africa

2 2nd Reading Ask and Answer Questions

Page 140: Wangari Maathai thought it was not fair that

____

______________________________.

Page 142: Deforestation caused water to dry up because

____

______________________________.

Page 143: Maathai thought that women would want to help because

______________________________.

3 3rd Reading Critical Thinking

Page 141: Tree roots were important for helping crops grow because

____

______________________________.

Page 144: The Tree Mother of Africa is a good nickname for Wangari Maathai because

____

______________________________.

Lesson 6

Science Texts

When you read a **science text**, you read true information about a science topic. In this lesson, you'll read three science texts about rain forests.

Skills Focus

- Connect Ideas
- Science Terms
- Text Features
- Compare and Contrast
- Roots and Prefixes
- Diagrams

Connect Ideas

Informational text has many ideas about a topic. Some of the ideas in a text go together. **Connecting ideas** means reading carefully to link one idea with another. This helps you understand more about what you are reading.

Let's Try It Read this paragraph.

People and animals breathe in oxygen from the air. Their bodies use the oxygen to make energy. Then people and animals breathe out carbon dioxide. Plants use carbon dioxide to make their food. Plants need the carbon dioxide to grow.

Underline the text that tells why people and animals need oxygen. Double underline the text that tells what happens after people and animals exhale carbon dioxide.

Discuss Why are people and animals important for plants?

Science Terms

A **science term** is a word or phrase that is important for understanding a science topic. Science terms are often in bold print.

Let's Try It

Read these sentences.

> Plants and trees make up different parts of the rain forest. These parts are called **layers**.

To learn what *layers* means, reread the words in the first sentence. Underline the context clues for *layers*.

Practice

Find these science terms in "The Tropical Rain Forest," the selection you are going to read. Use context clues to figure out each meaning. Circle the meaning below each term that makes the most sense.

1. **habitat,** page 162

   a place where an animal lives
   a layer of the rain forest

2. **understory,** page 164

   the layer above the canopy
   the layer below the canopy

Read for a Purpose

1 1st Reading

2 2nd Reading

3 3rd Reading

Read along with your teacher. Each time, read for a different purpose. Use the Tools on pages 187 and 188 as you read.

The Tropical Rain Forest

How do you know tropical rain forests are hot and wet?

A rain forest is wet. It has some of the wettest habitats on Earth. A **habitat** is a place where a plant or an animal lives. A habitat has everything the plant or animal needs to stay alive. Some rain forest habitats have the same weather almost every day.

Circle the words in bold print in the second paragraph. What does this term mean?

Many rain forests are hot. They are also very wet. They get more than 70 inches of rain every year. In some rain forests, it is about 80 degrees all year long. These places are called **tropical rain forests**.

The Layers of the Rain Forest

Plants and trees make up different parts of the rain forest. These parts are called **layers**. Sunlight helps form these layers. All plants need sunlight to live. The more sunlight a layer gets, the more its plant life grows.

In the rain forest, the tops of the trees get the most sunlight. So the treetops are very thick. This top layer is called the **canopy**. It covers the rain forest below. In fact, the canopy blocks most of the sunlight from reaching the layers below it. That makes the lower parts dark.

Why are the treetops in the canopy very thick?

Circle the subhead. What is this part of the article about?

The canopy trees are around 100 feet tall or even taller.

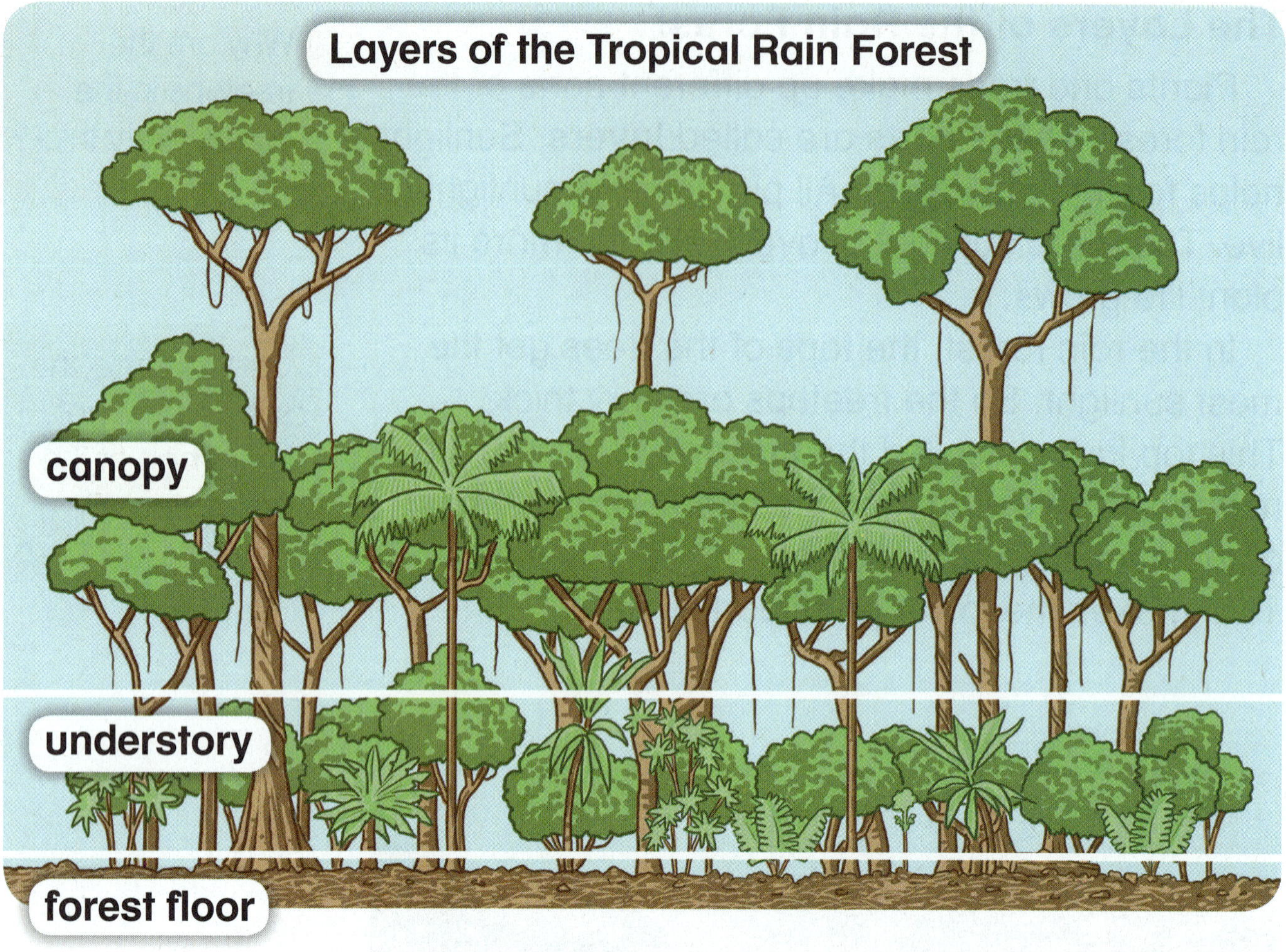

The **understory** is the next layer. It is below the canopy but above the ground. The understory does not get much sunlight. So fewer plants grow there. These plants do not need a lot of sunlight. Ferns are plants that grow in this layer.

The bottom layer is called the **forest floor**. The forest floor gets almost no sunlight. It is made up mainly of dead leaves. They come from trees and plants above.

How do saplings get enough sunlight?

Strong winds may blow down old trees. This makes holes in the canopy. The holes allow sunlight to reach the forest floor. Then new trees can grow on the forest floor. These young trees are called **saplings**. Saplings will only grow if they get enough sunlight. Then they may become tall canopy trees.

Rain Forest Animals

Millions of animals live in rain forests. Most live in the canopy. Many of these animals seldom leave the canopy. Everything they need to stay alive is there. There are fruits, leaves, and other animals to eat.

The sloth lives in tree branches. Its home is the understory and canopy. Sloths mostly eat leaves. Sloths' brown fur helps them hide. They seem to disappear in the trees.

The forest floor is also home to wildlife. Ants and beetles crawl through the dead leaves. Some of the biggest animals in the rain forest also live here. One of these is a large, spotted cat called the jaguar.

Circle the caption. What does this text tell you about sloths and jaguars?

Why might some rain forest animals seldom leave the canopy?

▼ Jaguars roam the forest floor. They also climb trees. Sloths are almost always in trees.

Rain Forests in Danger

Today, tropical rain forests are in danger. Some people cut down the trees to sell them. People also clear the land for farms or for roads.

Many people are working to save Earth's rain forests. They know that rain forests are important to us all. Rain forest plants help keep Earth's air healthy for living things. Some rain forest plants provide food for the world. Other plants are used to make medicines. If the rain forests are cut down, all these things could disappear.

What might happen to rain forest animals if the rain forests disappear?

▶ Many rain forest habitats are disappearing.

Check off after each reading. 1st Reading 2nd Reading 3rd Reading

Text Features

Text features are special parts of text that make it easier for readers to read and understand the text.

- A **subhead** is a title for a section of text.
- **Bold print** is darker than the text around it. Important words are often in bold print.
- A **caption** is a phrase or a sentence that tells more about a drawing or photograph.

Let's Try It Read this paragraph from an article about recycling.

Something Old Becomes New

When people **recycle**, they send old used products to a place where they are made new again. People throw away a lot of paper. But paper can be recycled. Recycling one ton of paper can save 17 trees.

▲ Old paper products can be recycled to make new paper products.

Circle the subhead, the caption, and the bold print.

Discuss How does each of the text features help you understand the paragraph?

Comprehension Check

1. How does sunlight help form the layers of the rain forest?

2. What information do the captions add to the selection?

3. Read these sentences from the selection.

   Then new trees can grow on the forest floor. These young trees are called saplings.

   Circle the word or words that help you understand the meaning of *saplings*. Then write the meaning of the word.

Respond to Text: Judge

Use the information from the text to think about cause and effect. Then make judgments about what you read.

Let's Try It What might happen to the rain forest if it is cut down? How might this change the world?

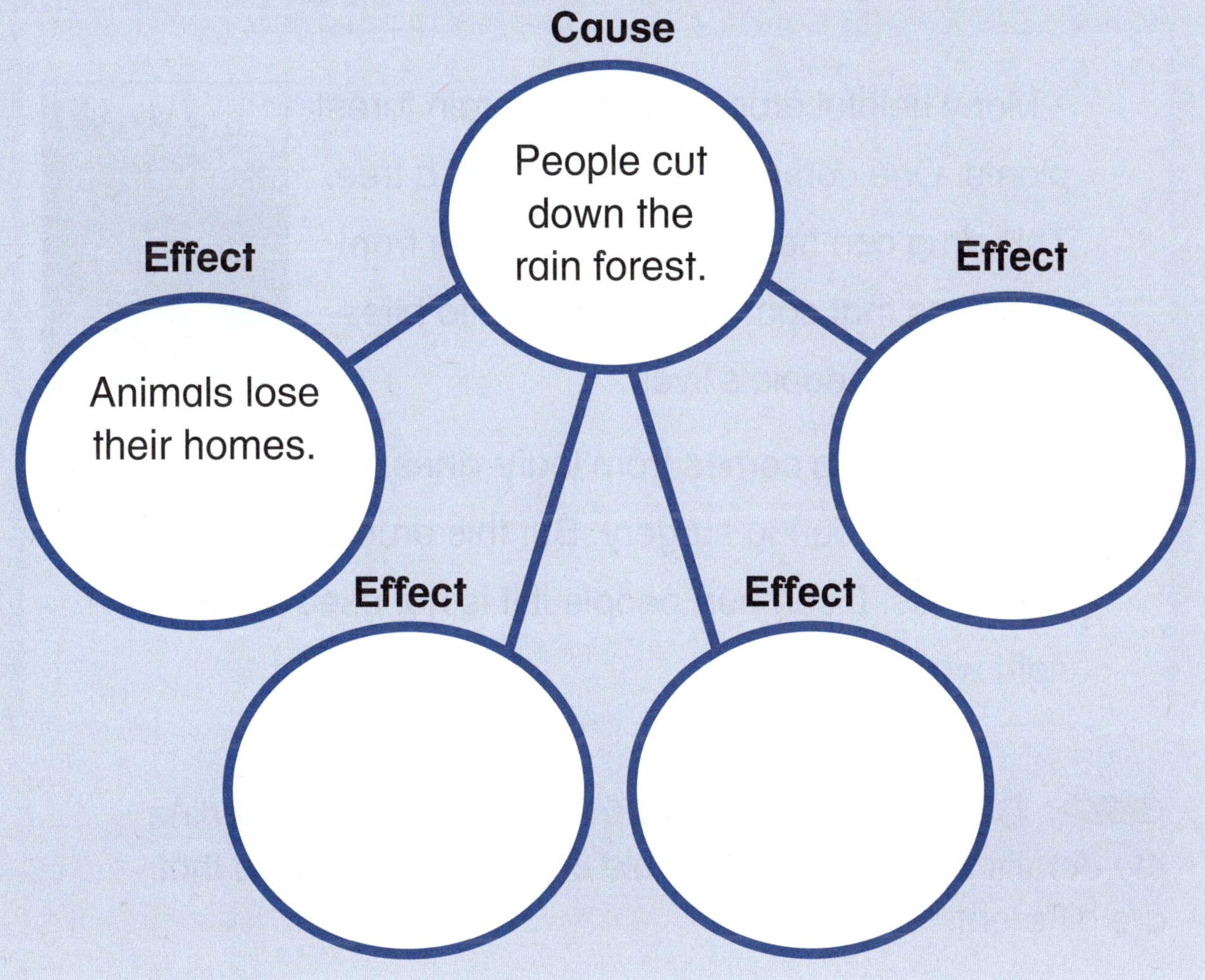

On Your Own

Should the rain forests be saved? Write a short paragraph that gives your opinion about this. Use what you wrote on this page and in your Tools on pages 187–188.

✔ Compare and Contrast

When you **compare** two things, you look at how they are alike. When you **contrast** two things, you look at how they are different.

Let's Try It Read these two paragraphs.

Many helpful drugs come from rain forest plants. One comes from the bark of a tree. This drug can help keep people safe from an illness that comes from mosquito bites. It can save people's lives.

Another drug comes from leafy vines. It can keep people safe during surgery. But this drug can be poisonous. It can hurt people if it is not used in the right way.

Compare and contrast these two drugs. Underline the details that are alike. Double underline the details that are different.

Discuss What are two ways that these drugs are alike? What is one way that they are different?

Roots and Prefixes

A **prefix** is a word part that is added to the beginning of a root word. Adding a prefix to a root word creates a new word with a new meaning.

The prefix *dis-* means "not" or "the opposite of."

The prefix *mis-* means "not" or "wrong."

Let's Try It Read the root word. What does it mean? Now add the prefix. What is the meaning of the new word?

Root Word	Prefix	New Word	Meaning
obey	dis-	disobey	not obey
spell	mis-	misspell	spell wrong

Practice

Read each sentence below. Circle the prefix in each underlined word. Then read the two meanings below the sentence. Circle the correct meaning of the word.

1. Some people misunderstand what the rain forest is like.

incorrectly understand   understand well

2. During evaporation, water seems to disappear.

appear again   go away

Read for a Purpose

1 1st Reading
2 2nd Reading
3 3rd Reading

Read along with your teacher. Each time, read for a different purpose. Use the Tools on pages 189 and 190 as you read.

What Puts the Rain in the Rain Forest?

Why is the rain forest a good place to see the water cycle in action?

What makes a rain forest different from other forests? It's the rain, of course! Some rain forests get rain nearly every day. Rain helps rain forest trees and plants grow. Their roots soak up the rain. The ground is almost always wet. Some people **misunderstand** what a rain forest is like. It is wet almost all the time!

All that rain makes the rain forest a great place to see how the water cycle works. The water cycle is the way water moves from the land to the air and back to the land. One event leads to another event. The events never stop. They are all connected. Nothing **disconnects** them.

The Water Cycle

Water in rivers, lakes, and oceans is a liquid. During the steps in the water cycle, the liquid changes. It becomes a form of water you cannot see. It seems to **disappear**, but the water is still there. It is a gas called water vapor. The vapor floats into the sky. There it changes back to liquid water.

The liquid water forms clouds. Water from the clouds falls back to Earth as rain. The rain falls onto plants and trees. It falls into rivers, lakes, and oceans. Then the cycle starts again.

Water vapor forms when the sun heats liquid water. This is called *evaporation*. Also, plants and trees give off water vapor. This is called *transpiration*.

Circle the title of the diagram. What does the diagram show?

How the Water Cycle Works

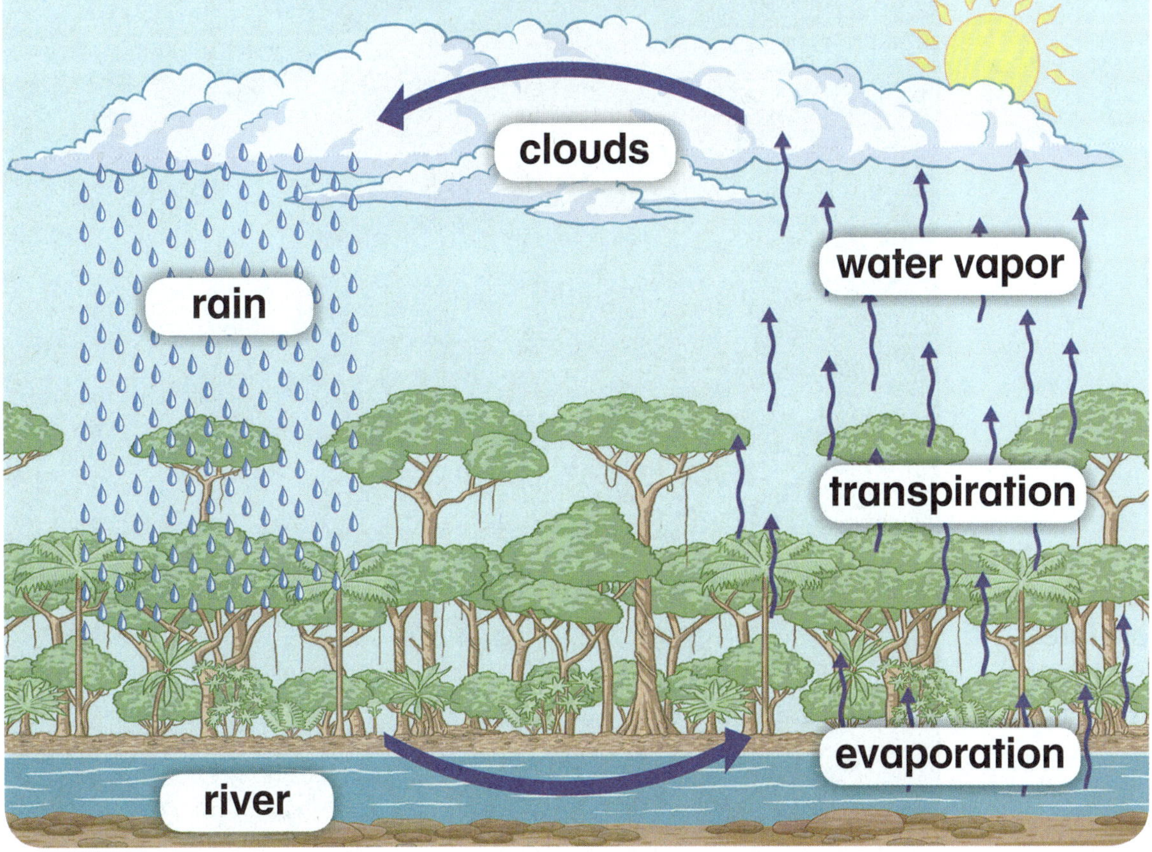

Changing Water into Vapor: Evaporation

During evaporation, the sun heats water. The water can be in lakes, ponds, oceans, or rivers. It can be the water on leaves after a rainfall. It can be water in puddles. As all this water gets warmer, some of it changes from liquid to water vapor.

The vapor floats into the sky. There the vapor cools off. It changes back into tiny droplets of liquid water. This change is called *condensation*. The droplets form clouds. Some of the droplets join together to form bigger drops. When the drops get big and heavy enough, they fall as rain.

▶ The sun heats the water in this river in the rain forest. Water is always evaporating from the river.

Changing Water into Vapor: Transpiration

Plants also send water vapor into the air. This part of the water cycle is called *transpiration*. Rainwater falls on the ground. Then the roots of plants and trees soak up the water.

Water travels up plant stems and tree trunks. The plants and trees use the water to help them grow. The water also carries nutrients from the soil.

The water reaches the leaves. The leaves let some of the water out through tiny holes. The water is vapor that goes into the air.

How are evaporation and transpiration alike?

Circle the title of the diagram. What does the diagram show about transpiration?

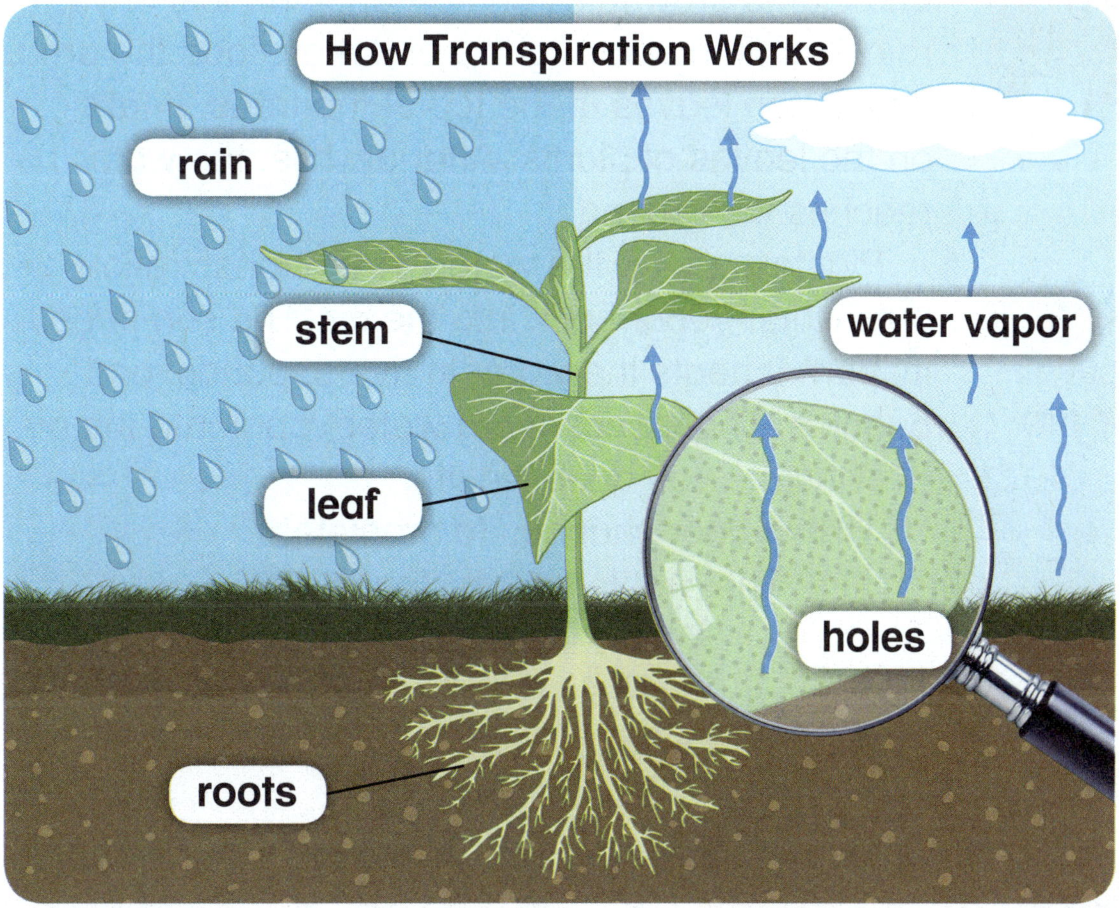

▶ Rain may fall lightly or heavily in the rain forest.

How does water get into the air in the rain forest water cycle?

How does the water cycle put the rain in the rain forest?

The Water Cycle in the Rain Forest

In the rain forest, the water cycle helps trees and plants grow thick and green. On most days, rain falls. It may fall lightly, or it may flood the area. It lands on leaves at the top of the trees. It falls on the leaves of plants. After a while, the water reaches the ground.

Plants soak up the water. Then transpiration puts water vapor back into the air. The sun does its part. It heats the water in rivers, ponds, and puddles. That sends more water vapor into the air.

Then . . . you guessed it!

The vapor changes to droplets.

The droplets form clouds.

Raindrops form from the droplets.

The rain falls in the rain forest.

And that's what puts the rain in the rain forest!

Check off after each reading. 1st Reading 2nd Reading 3rd Reading

Diagrams

A **diagram** is a drawing that shows the parts of something or how something works. A **title** tells what the diagram is about. **Labels** name parts of the diagram.

Let's Try It Read this diagram.

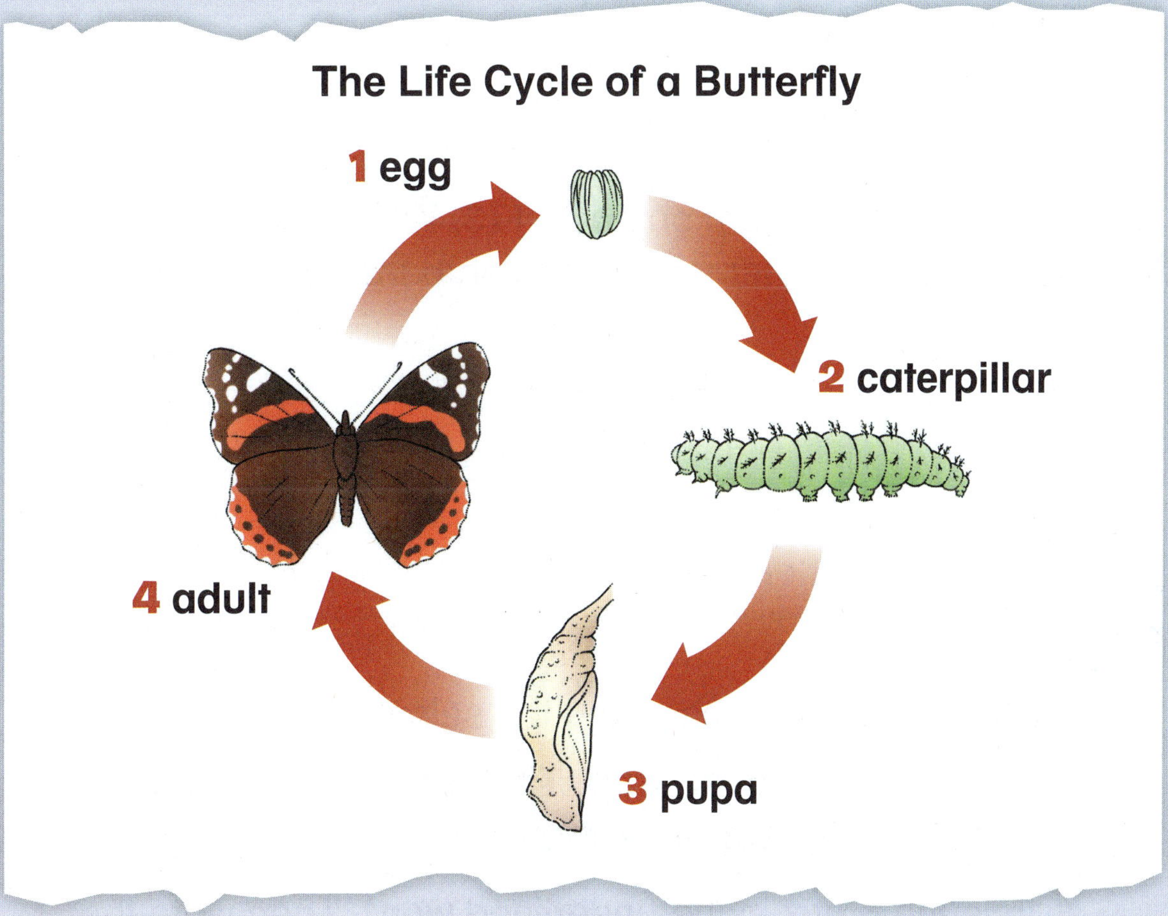

Underline the title. Circle the labels.

Discuss How do the labels help you know the order of the parts in the cycle?

Comprehension Check

1. How is rain different from water vapor? How are they alike?

2. Look at the diagram on page 173. What two things happen after water vapor floats into the sky?

3. Read these sentences from the selection.

   The events never stop. They are all connected. Nothing disconnects them.

   Circle the prefix in the underlined word. Then write the meaning of the word.

Respond to Text: Compare and Contrast

Use the information you learned from the two science texts about rain forests. Compare and contrast the information in the texts.

Let's Try It How are the details alike and different in these two science texts?

"The Tropical Rain Forest"	Both	"What Puts the Rain in the Rain Forest?"

On Your Own

Write a short paragraph to tell how "The Tropical Rain Forest" and "What Puts the Rain in the Rain Forest?" are alike. Tell how they are different, too. Support your answer with details. Use what you wrote on this page and your Tools on pages 187–190.

Take-Home Book

1. Remove this science text from your book.
2. Read it three times. Use what you have learned about science texts.

   1 1st Reading — Connect Ideas

   2 2nd Reading — Compare and Contrast

   3 3rd Reading — Critical Thinking
3. Answer the questions in the Comprehension Check on page 186.

Name: ______________________________

Read for a Purpose

Read the text three times. Use the skills you have learned. Then complete the Comprehension Check.

1 1st Reading
Connect Ideas

2 2nd Reading
Compare and Contrast

3 3rd Reading
Critical Thinking

The Red-Eyed Tree Frog

The rainy season has begun. Every leaf in the rain forest drips. Ponds fill up. Rivers flow faster. A red-eyed tree frog sits on a leaf. She has come down from high in the trees. She needs to be near water. It is time to lay her eggs.

Like all living things, a frog has a life cycle. A life cycle is made up of all the parts of an animal's life. A red-eyed tree frog goes through four stages. A stage is one part of a life cycle.

Why does the female frog come down near the water? Underline a sentence that tells you. This sentence has been underlined for you.

The Life Cycle of a Frog

Eggs

The cycle begins with eggs. A female red-eyed tree frog lays as many as 100 or more eggs. She lays them on a leaf. The leaf hangs over a pond or stream.

In a few days, the eggs hatch. The tree frog babies are called tadpoles. The liquid from inside the eggs causes the tadpoles to slide off the leaf. The tadpoles drop into the water below.

▲ Young frog tadpoles have eyes, a mouth, and a long tail.

▲ This frog tadpole has started to grow its hind legs.

Tadpoles

The tiny tadpoles look like fish. They have no legs. They have only a tail. They use their tails to swim. Like fish, they have gills. Gills let them breathe in the water.

At first, the tadpoles are weak. They hide near weeds or grass. Many fish would like to eat them.

The tadpoles eat tiny insects in and near the pond. The tadpoles grow and get stronger. When they are a few weeks old, they grow legs. First, the hind legs grow. Then the front legs grow.

How are tadpoles like fish? Circle the details in the text.

In what order do the tadpoles' legs grow? Underline the sentences that tell you.

Froglets

How are froglets different from tadpoles?

In a few more weeks, the tree frog tadpoles start to look like frogs. They are called froglets. They have bodies, legs, and feet. Now they have lungs. They can breathe on land. They are still brown. They still have tails.

The froglets' legs are strong enough to crawl. Froglets can go in and out of the water. The tail makes it hard to move on land. So froglets still spend time in the water.

When froglets are about 12 weeks old, their tails are gone. The froglets can climb trees. Little cups on their toes help them hang on.

▶ A tree frog froglet climbs on a leaf.

▲ An adult tree frog is about 3 inches long.

Adults

A few weeks later, the froglets are **adults**. They look just like their parents. The brown skin has become bright green. The tree frogs' sides have colorful blue stripes. Their feet are orange. Their eyes are bright red.

The adult frogs live high in the canopy. When they sleep, they tuck their legs in. This hides their bright colors. The frogs disappear into the leaves.

When the next rainy season comes, the red-eyed tree frogs climb down the trees. The females lay their eggs. The life cycle begins again.

What additional details would you use to explain the life cycle of the red-eyed tree frog?

Check off after each reading. 1st Reading 2nd Reading 3rd Reading

Comprehension Check

1. Look at the diagram on page 182. How does it help you understand the life cycle of a frog?

2. Under which subhead would you find information about where red-eyed tree frogs lay their eggs? What other information do you find there?

3. Read these sentences from the selection.

   A few weeks later, the froglets are adults. They look just like their parents.

   Circle the word or words that help you understand the meaning of *adults*. Then write the meaning.

Name: ____________________

The Tropical Rain Forest

1 1st Reading **Connect Ideas**

Page 162

Idea		Idea
Tropical rain forests are hot and wet.	→	

Page 163

Idea		Idea
	→	The treetops in the canopy are very thick.

Page 164

Idea		Idea
Saplings get enough sunlight.	→	

Name: ______________________________

The Tropical Rain Forest

2 2nd Reading Text Features

Page 162: Tropical rain forests are places where

____

______________________________.

Page 163: This part of the article is about

______________________________.

Page 165: The caption tells that

______________________________.

3 3rd Reading Critical Thinking

Page 165: Some animals seldom leave the canopy because

______________________________.

Page 166: If the rain forest disappears, rain forest animals

______________________________.

Name: ____

What Puts the Rain in the Rain Forest?

1 1st Reading **Compare and Contrast**

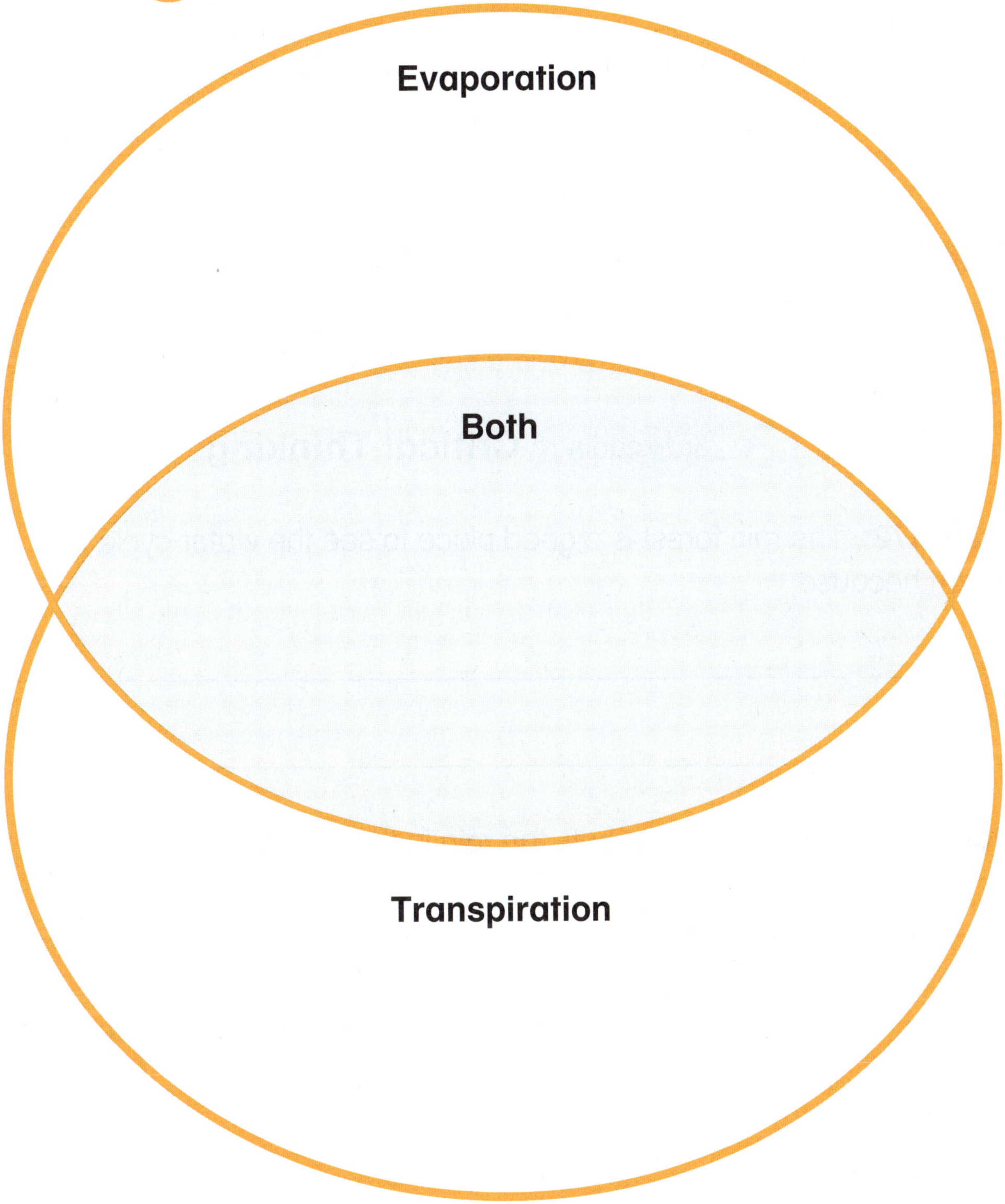

Name: ______________________________

What Puts the Rain in the Rain Forest?

2 2nd Reading Diagrams

Page 173: The diagram shows ______________________________

____.

Page 175: The diagram shows that transpiration ______________

____.

3 3rd Reading Critical Thinking

Page 172: The rain forest is a good place to see the water cycle in action because

____

____.

Page 176: The water cycle puts the rain in the rain forest because

____

____.

Lesson 7

Technical Texts

When you read a **technical text**, you read about how something works or how to do something. In this lesson, you will read three technical texts about how some foods are made.

Skills Focus

- Steps in a Process
- Multiple-Meaning Words
- Images
- Author's Purpose
- Root Words
- Text Features

Steps in a Process

Some informational texts explain how to make or do something. A **process** is a series of steps that take place to make or do something. The steps are in order from first to last.

Let's Try It Read this paragraph.

Here is one way that peanut butter is made. First, farmers send peanuts to a peanut butter factory. Next, the peanuts are roasted in a giant oven. Then a machine removes the skins from the peanuts. Finally, another machine grinds the peanuts into a butter.

Underline the sentence that tells you what process is explained. Circle the words that tell you the order of the steps.

Discuss In your own words, retell the process that is explained in the paragraph.

Multiple-Meaning Words

A **multiple-meaning word** is a word that has more than one meaning. You can use **context clues**, or the words near the multiple-meaning word, to figure out the correct meaning.

Let's Try It

Read the two definitions of the word *plant*. Then read the sentence.

plant ('plant) *noun.* **1:** a living thing that grows in the ground; **2:** a factory or place where something is made

At the **plant**, a machine crushes the tomatoes.

Underline the context clue in the sentence that helps you know what *plant* means. Then circle the definition that matches the meaning in the sentence.

Practice

Read the sentence. Circle the meaning of the word in **bold print**. Underline a context clue that helps you know the meaning.

1. The **belt** carries the tomatoes from one machine to the next.

   a strip of material that holds up pants

   a long band of material used to carry things in a factory

Read for a Purpose

1 1st Reading

2 2nd Reading

3 3rd Reading

Read along with your teacher. Each time, read for a different purpose. Use the Tools on pages 219 and 220 as you read.

Ketchup
From Farm to Kitchen

Where does the process of making ketchup start? Underline a sentence that tells you.

Ketchup is a very popular food. Every year, people buy millions of bottles of this tasty sauce.

Do you know where ketchup comes from? Every bottle starts with tomatoes. Tomatoes are the main ingredient. To become ketchup, tomatoes go through a special process.

Step 1: Growing

What happens to tomatoes right after they are picked? Circle the image that shows you. Describe the image you circled.

The process starts on tomato farms. Thousands of tomato plants grow in huge fields. Giant machines move through the fields. They pick the tomatoes. Then the tomatoes go into large boxes. The boxes go onto trucks. The trucks carry them to the next step.

Step 1: Growing

▶ On the farm, thousands of tomatoes are picked and ready to go to the next step.

Step 2: Cleaning

The next step in the process is at a factory. A company makes tomato **paste** there. Tomato paste is thick and smooth. Some food companies use tomato paste to make ketchup.

At the **plant**, tomatoes go onto wide **belts**. The belts carry the tomatoes from one machine to the next. First, the machines clean them. Next, workers remove any rotten tomatoes.

What is the order of the steps for cleaning the tomatoes? Underline words that help you follow the order.

Step 3: Crushing

The good, juicy tomatoes move to another part of the plant. There, a machine crushes them. The crushed tomatoes are called *pulp*. The pulp goes into large cooking kettles.

Circle the image that shows how tomatoes change in Step 3. How have these tomatoes changed?

Step 2: Cleaning

▲ Rotten tomatoes are removed from the healthy, ripe tomatoes.

Step 3: Crushing

▲ Crushed tomato pulp is chunky and juicy.

Why is tomato paste very thick?

Step 4: Making Tomato Paste

To make tomato paste, the crushed tomatoes need to be cooked. As they cook, most of the tomato juice boils away. Because it has less juice, the mixture turns into a paste. It has a **strong** tomato flavor. The tomatoes are now tomato paste.

Some factories put tomato paste in cans. They send it to stores. People buy it to make foods like spaghetti sauce.

This paste is going to become ketchup. Workers put the paste into big containers. Then they **ship** the containers to another factory. There, the paste will be made into ketchup.

Step 4: Making Tomato Paste

▲ Tomato paste is smoother and thicker than crushed tomatoes (above). Some companies sell tomato paste in cans (right).

Step 5: Mixing Ingredients

At the ketchup factory, a machine **feeds** the tomato paste into pipes. The pipes **shoot** the paste into large pots. The paste starts to cook again. Now, workers add special ingredients.

Most tomato ketchups have similar ingredients. These include salt, spices, and vinegar. The spices and salt are dry ingredients. Vinegar is a liquid.

Machines stir the ingredients. The mixture cooks for about an hour. That is just enough cooking time. Overcooking can ruin the taste. The cooked mixture is now ketchup. It flows through pipes to the next step.

Reread the first paragraph. What two events happen to change tomato paste to ketchup? Underline the text that tells you.

How does the tomato paste go from Step 5 to the next step? Circle the image that shows you.

Step 5: Mixing Ingredients

▲ Most kinds of ketchup have a secret mix of spices.

How have tomatoes changed by the time they become ketchup?

Step 6: Bottling

In the next step, bottling machines squirt the ketchup into bottles. Then labels go onto each bottle. Finally, the bottles go into boxes.

Trucks carry the boxes to stores all over the country. The stores sell the ketchup to customers.

At one store, a family buys a bottle.

Step 7: Eating!

The family brings the ketchup home. They'll add it to recipes. They'll pour it on sandwiches and other foods.

Where does the ketchup end up? In a hungry person's stomach, of course!

Step 6: Bottling

▲ Ketchup comes in bottles of different sizes and shapes.

Step 7: Eating!

▲ People eat ketchup on many different foods.

Check off after each reading. 1st Reading 2nd Reading 3rd Reading

Images

Informational texts often have images such as **photographs**, **drawings**, or **diagrams**. These images can show how a process works to help you better understand the text.

Let's Try It Look at the diagram. Then follow the directions.

Ketchup: From the Factory to the Store

Step 1: Into Boxes **Step 2: Onto Trucks** **Step 3: To the Store**

Underline the title of the diagram. Circle the labels that help you know the order of the steps.

Discuss Use the diagram to tell how ketchup goes from the factory to the store.

Comprehension Check

1. Cooking happens two times in the process of making ketchup. In which steps does cooking happen?

2. Look at page 194. How does the large picture of many tomatoes help you understand where tomatoes come from?

3. Read this sentence from the selection.

   Then they ship the containers to another factory.

   Circle the meaning of *ship* that matches the meaning in the sentence.

   a large boat   to send something somewhere

Respond to Text: Compare

The process of making ketchup includes the process of making tomato paste. Tomato paste has to be made before ketchup can be made. Some of the steps are the same in each process.

Let's Try It Write down ways in which making tomato paste and ketchup are similar and different.

Making Tomato Paste	Both	Making Ketchup
Starts with . . .	Use . . .	Starts with . . .
Liquid is . . .	Happen in . . .	Liquid is . . .
	Use big pots to . . .	

On Your Own

Write a short paragraph that explains how these two processes are similar. Support your answer with details. You can use what you wrote on this page and in your Tools on pages 219–220.

Author's Purpose

Authors of informational texts have different purposes for writing. The **author's purpose** is the reason why the author wrote the text.

Let's Try It Read this paragraph.

Fruit Juice Ice Cubes

Making fruit juice ice cubes is really easy. Here is how to do it. First, pour a glass of your favorite juice. Next, take an empty ice cube tray. Pour the juice in the tray. Now, put the tray inside a freezer. After 2–3 hours, remove the tray from the freezer. Now you have a tasty frozen treat!

Underline two sentences that tell you the author will be explaining something.

Discuss Why does this author say that making fruit juice ice cubes is really easy?

Root Words

A **root word** is the main part of a word that tells the word's meaning. If you do not know the meaning of a longer word, you may be able to use its root word to figure out the meaning.

Let's Try It Read each new word. Then read the root word.

New Word	Root Word	Meaning
mostly	most	for the most part
lumpy	lump	filled with lumps

Circle the root word in each new word. How does the root word help you figure out the meaning of the new word?

Practice

Read each sentence. Circle the root word in each underlined word. Then write the meaning of the underlined word.

1. Some bacteria are dangerous and can make people sick.

____

2. Finally, thick, creamy butter remains.

____

Read for a Purpose

1 1st Reading

2 2nd Reading

3 3rd Reading

Read along with your teacher. Each time, read for a different purpose. Use the Tools on pages 221 and 222 as you read.

Made with Milk

What does the author want you to know about milk? Underline two sentences in the first paragraph that tell you.

Milk is not just for drinking. It is the main ingredient in a number of delicious foods, too. Butter comes from milk. So do cheese and ice cream. Foods made from milk are called *dairy products*.

Most dairy products start with cows. Cows make milk inside their bodies. Today, most cow's milk comes from farms. Farmers send the milk to dairy companies. These companies make dairy products. They use a different process for each food.

Circle the caption. What does it tell you about the photograph?

All these products are made with milk.

Butter

Fresh cow's milk has two main parts. One is called *cream*. Cream is **mostly** fat. The other is *skim milk*.

Companies use cream in the process for making butter. First, a machine stirs cream in a large container. This is called *churning*. Churning makes the fat stick together. It also removes a liquid called *buttermilk*. **Finally**, thick, creamy butter remains.

What does the author want you to understand in the second paragraph? Underline a sentence that tells you.

Circle the subhead. What does it tell you about the information on this page?

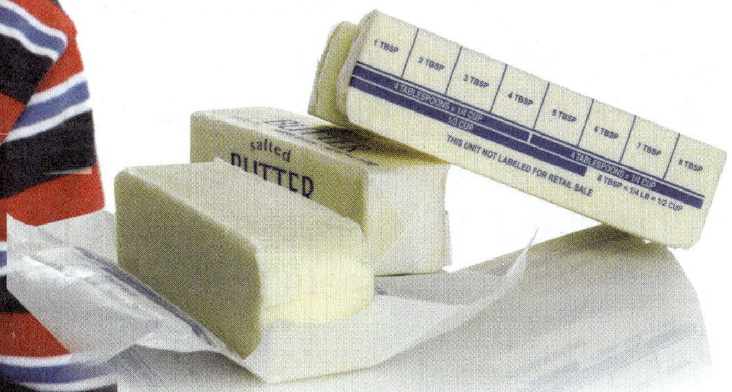

▼ At the store, butter usually comes in sticks.

▶ Cheese is in many foods, including pizza.

Circle the caption. What additional information does it give you about cheese?

How did cheese help solve the problem of wasting milk?

Cheese

If milk is not kept cold, it spoils. That means you can't drink it anymore. This can be **wasteful**. People long ago figured out a process to solve this problem. They made cheese. Cheese lasts a long time without spoiling.

To make some hard cheeses, people add bacteria to milk. Bacteria are tiny living things. Some are germs. They can make people sick. But others are not **dangerous**. Cheese companies use these safe bacteria. The bacteria help form **lumpy** substances in the milk. These are called *curds*. Cheese makers remove the curds. Then they cook them. Finally, they form the curds into blocks. Over time, these blocks change into cheese.

Ice Cream

Ice cream is one of the sweetest dairy products. In the United States, people eat millions of gallons of ice cream each year.

The main ingredient in ice cream is cream. First, ice cream makers mix cream and sugar together. Sometimes they add egg yolks. They also add flavorings such as fruit and spices. They heat the mixture. Finally, it goes into large containers. The containers stay very cold.

A machine stirs the mixture. Stirring keeps it from freezing into a solid chunk. Stirring also prevents ice from forming in the cream. The mixture thickens. Before long, the creamy, smooth ice cream is ready to eat.

Why did the author include a fact about how many gallons of ice cream people eat each year?

Why does the author write about other kinds of milk? Underline a sentence that tells you.

Why do you think people in other parts of the world use different animals for milk and dairy products?

Not Just Cow's Milk

Around the world, people use different kinds of milk to make dairy products. Some people make goat's milk ice cream. Others eat reindeer cheese. Others cook with yak butter.

Whatever milk they use, the processes for making dairy products are all similar. In the end, the result is something **milky** and delicious for the people who eat it.

▶ People in parts of Asia make butter from yak milk. A yak is an animal that is similar to a cow.

Check off after each reading. 1st Reading 2nd Reading 3rd Reading

✔ Text Features

Text features are parts of a text that make it easier for readers to read and find information. A **subhead** is a title for a section of text. A **caption** is a phrase or a sentence that tells more about a drawing or photograph.

Let's Try It Read this article.

Food from Italy

A number of foods we eat come from Italy. Italy is a country in Europe.

Pizza

Pizza is made with dough, tomato sauce, and cheese. First, you shape the dough into a flat pie. Then you cover it with tomato sauce and cheese. Finally, you bake it in an oven for about 20 minutes.

▲ Sprinkle the cheese on top of the tomato sauce.

Circle the subhead. Underline the caption.

Discuss What does the caption tell you about making pizza?

Comprehension Check

1. Reread page 208. What is the author's purpose for including the section "Not Just Cow's Milk"?

2. Reread the caption on page 208. How does the caption support the main text?

3. Read this sentence from the selection.

   In the end, the result is something milky and delicious for the people who eat it.

   Circle the root word in the underlined word. Then write the meaning of the underlined word.

Respond to Text: Compare and Contrast

"Ketchup: From Farm to Kitchen" and "Made with Milk" both tell about how foods are made. **Compare** and **contrast** the information in these two texts.

Let's Try It

What do the texts tell you about how foods are made? How are the details in the texts alike? How are they different?

"Ketchup: From Farm to Kitchen"	Both	"Made with Milk"

On Your Own

Write a short paragraph that tells how the processes in "Ketchup: From Farm to Kitchen" and "Made with Milk" are similar and different. Support your answer with details. You can use what you wrote on this page and in your Tools on pages 219–222.

Take-Home Book

1. Remove this technical text from your book.
2. Read it three times. Use what you have learned about technical texts.

   1 1st Reading — Steps in a Process

   2 2nd Reading — Author's Purpose

   3 3rd Reading — Critical Thinking

3. Answer the questions in the Comprehension Check on page 218.

Name: ____________________

Read for a Purpose

Read the text three times. Use the skills you have learned. Then complete the Comprehension Check.

1 1st Reading
Steps in a Process

2 2nd Reading
Author's Purpose

3 3rd Reading
Critical Thinking

Rainbow Fruit Sticks

These rainbow snacks are made with fruit. They have all the colors of the rainbow. They certainly are tasty. They are beautiful, too. And they are healthy. You will need an adult to help you cut the fruit.

Best of all, the process is simple. Rainbow fruit sticks are fun to make!

What does the author most want you to know about making rainbow fruit snacks? Double underline two sentences that tell you. The first sentence has been underlined for you.

What is the first step for making rainbow fruit sticks? Underline two clues that tell you.

Step 1: Gather Ingredients and Equipment

Make sure that you have all of the ingredients and equipment that you need to make this recipe.

- 6 different colors of fruits
- 6 wooden sticks or skewers
- 6 small bowls
- a sink
- paper towels
- a knife
- a cutting board
- a serving dish

Ingredients

Here are some colorful fruit ideas. Remember, you need 6 colors.

Equipment

6 small bowls

skewers

knife

cutting board

serving dish

Step 2: Wash the Fruit

First, you need to wash the fruit. That will make it safe to eat. It will help remove dirt and germs from the fruit's skin.

Rinse each piece of fruit under the faucet.

Next, dry the fruit with paper towels. Now you are ready for the next step.

What do you do with the fruit in Step 2? Underline the words that tell you the order.

◀ Wash the fruit carefully.

What does the author want you to know about grapes and berries? Double underline two sentences that help you know.

Step 3: Cut the Fruit

The next step is to cut the fruit. Only an adult should use sharp cutting tools.

Use the knife and cutting board. Slice each piece of fruit. Cut them into bite-sized chunks. Be **careful** when you cut apples or plums. Make sure there is some skin on each piece. That will show the rainbow color. You can keep grapes and berries whole. They are already bite-sized!

Put the pieces in the six small bowls. Use one bowl for each color of fruit.

▶ Cut the fruit into pieces that will only take one bite to eat.

Step 4: Put It All Together

Have an adult help you put the fruit on the wooden skewers. Here is the order for the fruit. You want to make a rainbow!

purple blue green yellow orange red

Follow the same process with five more sticks. Display them on a dish.

Which step do you think would be the easiest to do? Which step would be the hardest? Why?

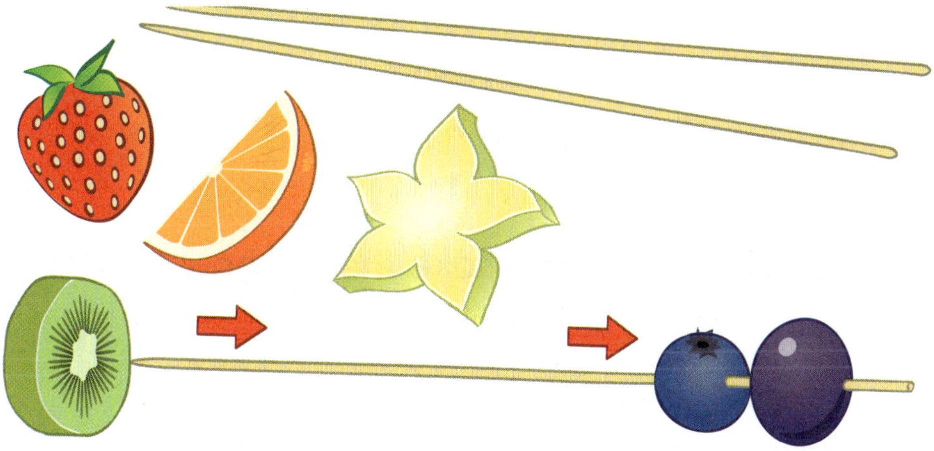

Step 5: Enjoy!

Invite friends to share. Take the snacks to school. Eat, laugh, and have a colorful blast!

Check off after each reading. 1st Reading 2nd Reading 3rd Reading

Comprehension Check

1. Look at the pictures on page 214. How do they help you understand which colors of fruit you will need?

2. How do the subheads help you make the rainbow fruit sticks?

3. Read these sentences from the selection.

Be careful when you cut apples or plums. Make sure there is some skin on each piece. That will show the rainbow color.

Circle the root word in the underlined word. Then write the meaning of the underlined word.

Name: ______________________________

Ketchup: From Farm to Kitchen

1 1st Reading **Steps in a Process**

Page 194

The process starts . . .

Page 195

The steps for cleaning are . . .

First . . .

Next . . .

Page 197

The two events that happen to change tomato paste to ketchup are . . .

1.

2.

Name: ____________________

Ketchup: From Farm to Kitchen

2 2nd Reading Images

Page 194: The image shows

____________________.

Page 195: The image shows that in Step 3, the tomatoes

____

____________________.

Page 197: The image shows that between Step 5 and Step 6, the ketchup

____________________.

3 3rd Reading Critical Thinking

Page 196: Tomato paste is very thick because

____________________.

Page 198: By the time tomatoes become ketchup, they have

____

____________________.

Name: ______________________________

Made with Milk

1 1st Reading **Author's Purpose**

Author's Purpose	Clues from the Text
Page 204 The author wants me to know that milk . . .	I know this because the author writes . . .
Page 205 The author wants me to understand . . .	I know this because the author writes . . .
Page 207 The author wants to explain . . .	I know this because the author includes a fact about how much ice cream people eat each year.
Page 208 The author wants to show . . .	The author writes about milk from animals that are not cows.

Name: ____________________

Made with Milk

2 2nd Reading Text Features

Page 204: The caption tells me that the photograph

____________________.

Page 205: The subhead tells me that this page explains

____________________.

Page 206: The caption tells that

____________________.

3 3rd Reading Critical Thinking

Page 206: Cheese helped solve the problem of wasting milk because

____

____________________.

Page 208: People in other parts of the world use different animals for milk and dairy products because

____

____________________.

Lesson 8

Opinion

An **opinion** is a text that tells what the author thinks or believes about a topic. In this lesson, you will read three different opinions about pets.

Skills Focus

- Main Topic
- Real-Life Connections
- Author's Purpose
- Compare and Contrast
- Shades of Meaning
- Support for Author's Points

Main Topic

An opinion text usually gives an opinion about one main topic. The **main topic** is what the text is mostly about. **Supporting paragraphs** tell more about the main topic.

Let's Try It Read this opinion text.

Of all birds, parrots make the worst pets. My family once had a parrot, and we had problems with him.

Parrots are noisy. They can imitate many sounds, such as people talking. So they learn to say words. Our parrot never stopped talking!

Parrots live too long. Some live as long as 80 years. Who wants to hear the same noisy bird for that long?

What is the main topic of this text? Underline a sentence in the first paragraph that tells what the text is mostly about.

Discuss How does the second paragraph support the main topic? How does the third paragraph support the same main topic?

✔ Real-Life Connections

You can make a **real-life connection** between a word and the world. When you make the connection, you think of people or events in life that show the meaning of the word.

Let's Try It

Read these sentences.

As puppies grow older, they become **curious**. They want to explore their world.

Make a connection between the word *curious* and real life. Underline text that gives a real-life connection. How would you describe people or animals that are curious?

Practice

Read each sentence below. Then answer the question.

1. Young dogs need to learn how to **behave** correctly.

   How might a real dog behave correctly?

   ____

   ____

2. With time, puppies learn to **obey**.

   How would a puppy obey someone?

   ____

   ____

Read for a Purpose

1 1st Reading

2 2nd Reading

3 3rd Reading

Read along with your teacher. Each time, read for a different purpose. Use the Tools on pages 251 and 252 as you read.

What is this page mostly about? Underline two sentences in the second paragraph that best show how the author feels about the main topic.

The Happy Dogs Blog

May I Suggest a Puppy?

by Juanita Burrows

We all know that dogs are great pets. Dogs can learn tricks. They make loving friends. They are wonderful **companions**. A dog can even **protect** you. So what do you do when you want a new dog?

To start, you need to make choices. Do you want a beagle? Do you want a golden retriever? Will it be another breed of dog? Next, there is another important choice to make. Will you get a puppy or an adult dog? I suggest a puppy. A puppy is the best choice.

puppy

adult

Which will you choose?

There are obvious reasons to pick a puppy. Puppies are fun! They are cute. They love to play. They are so small. You can pick up most puppies and carry them anywhere you happen to go.

But there are other important reasons to pick a puppy. One, I have found that puppies are easier to train than adult dogs. Two, *you* get to train a puppy. You don't have to teach an old dog new tricks.

Puppies are the best choice!

Underline a sentence that tells what the first paragraph is mostly about. What is an obvious reason to pick a puppy?

What is the author's purpose for writing the second paragraph? Circle a sentence that tells you.

What is this page mostly about? Underline a sentence that tells you.

Why does the author include details about when puppies become curious? Circle a sentence that tells what the author wants to explain.

The most important reason you should get a puppy is that they are usually easy to train. Young dogs need to learn how to **behave**. Until they are about 1 month old, puppies mostly stay with their mothers. When they are between 1 and 3 months old, they become **curious**. They want to explore their world. They want to learn. They are ready to form a close friendship with a human owner. This is the age when dogs learn things most easily. That means young dogs can be easier to train than older dogs.

Puppies are ready to learn.

Puppies have a lot to learn. With time, they learn to **obey**. They can learn to sit and stay quietly. They can learn to walk on a leash. They can learn not to chew your sneakers or the couch.

It is my experience that older dogs can be harder to train. Many older dogs come from other homes. They have had previous owners. An older dog may have bad habits, like chewing things and barking a lot. It can take a lot of extra time to teach them good behaviors.

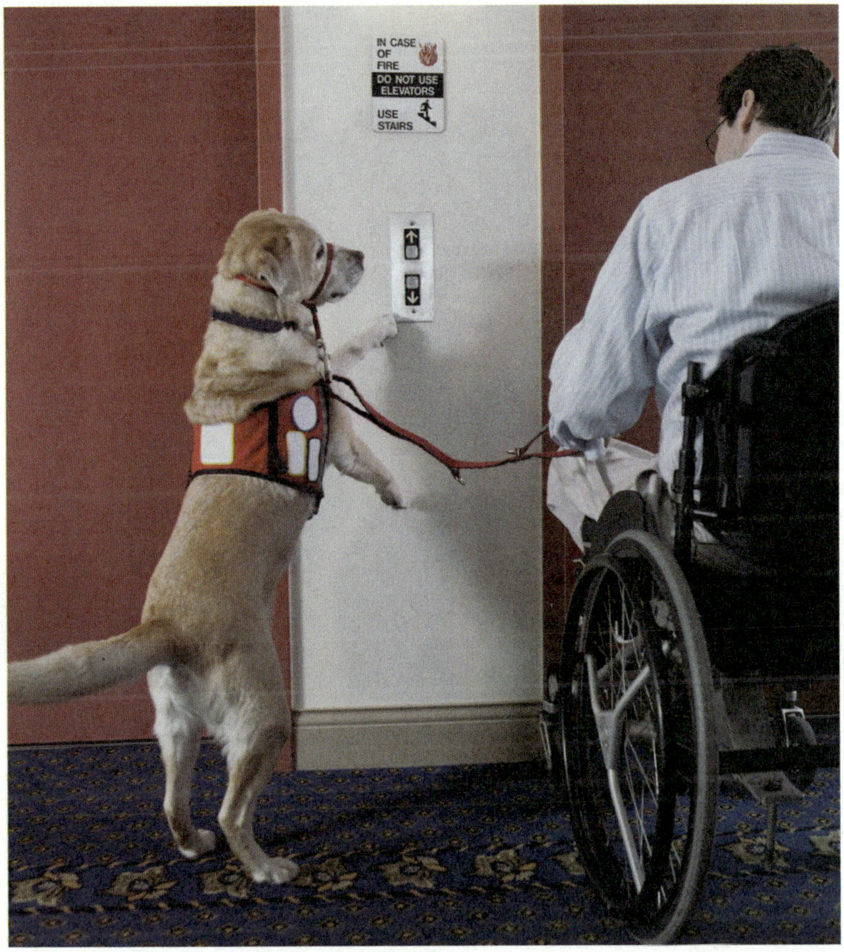

Some service dogs start to learn as puppies.

What is the second paragraph mostly about? Underline a sentence that tells you.

Why do the words "my experience" help you know that this is the author's opinion?

Why does the author write that "*you* get to do the training"?

Why does training form a special bond between you and your puppy?

There's another good reason to get a puppy. With a puppy, *you* get to do the training. You are a puppy's first trainer. Hopefully, you will be its only trainer for life. You teach the puppy what you want it to learn. You don't have to fix problems caused by other owners. Plus, training forms a special bond between you and your puppy. You will become close friends.

A puppy is certainly the best choice. Pick a puppy. Both you and your new furry friend will be very happy!

Check off after each reading. 1st Reading 2nd Reading 3rd Reading

✔ Author's Purpose

Authors of informational texts have different purposes for writing. The **author's purpose** is the reason why the author wrote the text.

Let's Try It Read this paragraph.

Here is why I love cats. First, cats are sweet and cuddly. Second, cats are easy. You don't have to take a cat for a walk twice a day. People with dogs have to do that. Third, cats are quiet. They don't bark. This is why you should get a cat!

Underline a sentence that tells what the author wants the reader to know.

Discuss What does the author want the reader to do? Why does the author want the reader to do this?

Comprehension Check

1. Reread page 230. How does the first paragraph support the main topic of the whole text?

2. Reread page 229. What is the author's purpose for writing the second paragraph?

3. Read this sentence.

   Puppies make loving friends. They are wonderful companions.

   Circle a word in the first sentence that helps you know the meaning of *companion*. What does someone do when he or she is a good companion?

Respond to Text: Evaluate

The author of "May I Suggest a Puppy?" tells her opinion about pet dogs. Use details from the selection to evaluate her opinion.

Let's Try It

Here are three of the reasons that the author gives to support her opinion. Next to each reason, write what you think about that reason. The first one is an example of what you might write.

Reasons to Get a Puppy	What You Think
Puppies are fun. They are cute. They like to play.	I think these are good examples of why a puppy is fun. It is fun to have a cute pet that plays with you.
Puppies are easy to train. They are curious.	
Older dogs may already behave badly.	

On Your Own

Do you agree with the author's opinion about puppies? Write a short paragraph that evaluates the author's opinion. Support your answer with details. Use what you wrote on this page and in your Tools on pages 251–252.

Compare and Contrast

When you **compare** two things, you look at how they are the same. When you **contrast** two things, you look at how they are different.

Let's Try It Read this story.

My brother has a pet lizard and a gerbil. I like the gerbil best. Both pets live in small spaces. Both pets eat vegetables and fruit. But the lizard eats live bugs! The bugs escape out of the tank. Plus, I like how the gerbil feels. Both pets are soft. But the gerbil is furry while the lizard is spiky.

Underline the text that tells how the lizard and gerbil are alike. Double underline the text that tells how they are different.

Discuss In what ways do the two pets feel the same to touch? In what ways do they feel different?

Shades of Meaning

Some words, like *big, enormous,* and *gigantic*, tell about a similar idea but have slightly different meanings. These small differences are called **shades of meaning**.

Let's Try It Read these sentences.

Most puppies are energetic. They run around the house like tiny, bouncy balls of destruction.

Circle the words that help you better understand what each underlined word means. How are the words *bouncy* and *energetic* similar? How are they different?

Practice

Read each pair of words. Circle the words that tell about the same idea but with a slightly different meaning. Then write one more word that belongs with the words you circled.

1. *sleepy* and *drowsy* *strange* and *heavy*

2. *happy* and *glad* *sad* and *funny*

3. *sweet* and *salty* *fun* and *exciting*

Read for a Purpose

1 1st Reading

2 2nd Reading

3 3rd Reading

Read along with your teacher. Each time, read for a different purpose. Use the Tools on pages 253 and 254 as you read.

Animal Adoption Center of Pleasantville

Animal Adoption Center Bulletin

Get an Older Dog!

by Arnold Enright

So, you're looking for a new dog. It's quite an adventure. Where will you find your new furry friend? An animal shelter has dogs of all breeds. Or you might go to a pet store.

Before you go, there is another important decision to make. Do you want a puppy or an older dog? Both can be wonderful companions.

But I believe that you should get an older dog. Here's why.

What is one way that older dogs and younger dogs are alike? Underline a clue in the second paragraph.

Think about the topic of this text. What is the author's opinion about this topic? Circle a sentence that tells you.

You'll be cleaning up after a puppy all the time.

Puppies Are Too Much Work

It's hard to resist puppies. They are **exciting** bundles of joy. But puppies are hard work. Most puppies are **energetic**. They run around the house like tiny, **bouncy** balls of destruction.

Puppies need more care than older dogs. They need attention as you train them. You have to walk and run them outside. Inside, they chew your shoes and the furniture. They cannot be left alone. It doesn't matter if it's the middle of the afternoon or the middle of the night. When a puppy needs to go for a walk, you have to go, too!

How are puppies different from older dogs? Underline a sentence that tells you.

Why are puppies too much work?

What is an important way in which older dogs are different from puppies? Underline a sentence that tells you.

The author says that older dogs can sit, stay, and be silent. What point do these reasons support?

Older dogs are just as much fun as puppies.

Many Older Dogs Are Well Behaved

Let's face it, older dogs are easier to live with. Many older dogs are already trained. They know how to behave. They can be left alone. When you return home, you won't walk in on a disaster. Older dogs can walk on a leash. They know how to sit, stay, and be silent. They usually won't wake you up in the middle of the night.

And just because an older dog is well behaved doesn't mean it won't be **fun**. Just like puppies, they can learn tricks. They can learn to fetch balls. And they are very loyal. They'll stay by your side.

There are too many older dogs in shelters.

Older Dogs Need You!

The most important reason for getting an older dog is that older dogs need you. Most shelters are full of dogs. They all need homes. But people always seem to want puppies. So puppies seem to get picked first. They don't stay in shelters very long. Older dogs often stay longer. They can get lonely and sad.

Why are older dogs in shelters? Maybe a family moved to a new apartment that does not allow dogs. Maybe an owner could no longer take care of a dog. So people leave their dogs at shelters. They hope someone else will take care of their pets.

In what ways is life in an animal shelter different for older dogs and puppies? Underline the text that tells you.

On this page, the author says that older dogs are gentle and peaceful. Which point does this reason support? Circle a sentence that tells you.

Older Dogs Are Happy to Be with You

What is the best thing about older dogs? They are usually easy to be with. They are happy to be around people. They usually behave well around children and other pets. Older dogs have more experience. This can make them **gentle** and **peaceful**.

Older dogs need a human friend they can love. They will reward you with friendship, loyalty, and fun for the rest of their lives.

So, next time you're looking for a new furry friend, pick an older dog. You'll be glad you did.

Why would it be important for a dog to be gentle and peaceful?

Check off after each reading.

1st Reading

2nd Reading

3rd Reading

Support for Author's Points

An author of an opinion text tells how he or she thinks or feels about a topic. He or she makes **points** to support that opinion. An author includes **reasons** to support each point.

Let's Try It Read this paragraph.

I believe the octopus is the most interesting animal in the ocean. First, an octopus is smart. Some octopuses collect coconut shells to use as tools. Second, an octopus has amazing skin. Some octopuses can change their skin colors. Finally, they shoot out a black, inky substance when they are in danger. It helps them get away from attackers.

Underline the author's opinion. Then double underline three points that the author makes.

Discuss What reasons does the author give to support his or her points? Which point is best supported by its reason?

Comprehension Check

1. Reread page 238. According to the author, what is one way in which puppies and older dogs are similar?

2. Reread page 239. What reason does the author give to support his point that older dogs need you?

3. Read this sentence from the story.

   Older dogs have more experience. This can make them gentle and peaceful.

   Circle the two words that have similar meanings. Which of these words would best be used to describe a dog that seldom barks? Use that word in a sentence about a dog.

Respond to Text: Compare and Contrast

What are the authors' opinions in "May I Suggest a Puppy?" and "Get an Older Dog!"? Are the opinions the same or different?

Let's Try It List the main points from each text in the chart. Circle the points that are similar.

"May I Suggest a Puppy?"	"Get an Older Dog!"

On Your Own

After comparing and contrasting both selections, would you want to own a puppy or an older dog? Which author was more convincing? Write a paragraph that explains which opinion you agree with. Support your answer with details. Use what you wrote on this page and in your Tools on pages 251–254.

Take-Home Book

1. Remove this opinion text from your book.
2. Read it three times. Use what you have learned about opinions.

   1 1st Reading **Main Topic**

   2 2nd Reading **Compare and Contrast**

   3 3rd Reading **Critical Thinking**

3. Answer the questions in the Comprehension Check on page 250.

Name: ______________________________________

Read for a Purpose

Read the text three times. Use the skills you have learned. Then complete the Comprehension Check.

1 1st Reading
Main Topic

2 2nd Reading
Compare and Contrast

3 3rd Reading
Critical Thinking

The East End Animal Shelter

Adopt a Pet

Pet stores and animal shelters both have pets. But pet stores can be expensive. It is better to go to an animal shelter. There you can adopt a furry or feathered friend.

When you adopt, you take a shelter animal home with you. Shelter animals all need new homes. So stop at your local shelter. Adopt your next pet. It's always better to adopt.

What is the main topic of this page? Underline the sentence that tells you. This sentence is already underlined for you.

How are pet stores and animal shelters alike? Circle the sentence that tells you.

Why is it an act of kindness to adopt a pet from an animal shelter?

Point Number 1

First, there are too many pets in animal shelters today. Millions of animals live in shelters. Some have lost their owners. Others were given up for adoption. They all need new homes. It is an act of kindness to take one home.

Point Number 2

Second, you will know your pet is healthy. Shelters take good care of animals. Vets examine each animal carefully. A vet is an animal doctor. Vets make sure that pets are not sick. Shelters will not let you adopt a pet that isn't fit.

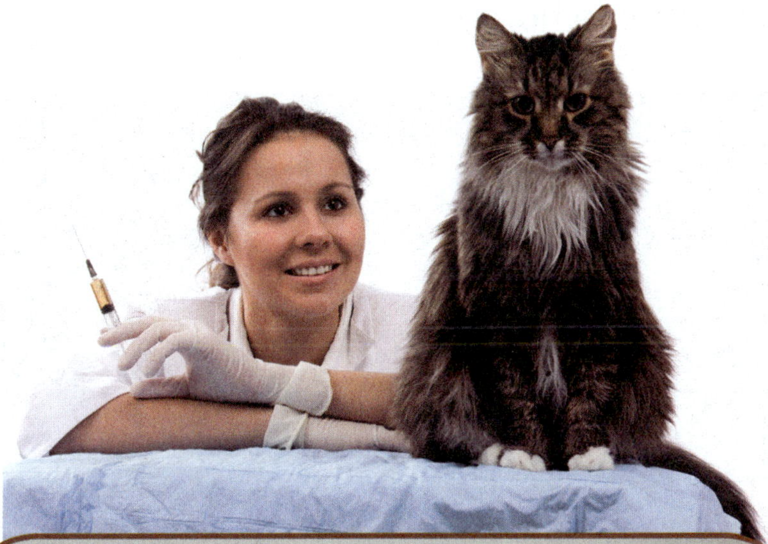

What is the main topic of this page? Underline a sentence that tells what this page is mostly about.

Why would it be better for an animal to go home with an owner than stay in an animal shelter?

Point Number 3

Third, you can save a pet from an unhappy life. Pets at shelters are healthy. They are well cared for. But they are not always happy. Shelters can be crowded. They can be noisy. This can be a problem for many animals. Give a pet a cozy, comfortable home!

Point Number 4

Finally, shelter pets don't cost much. People can pay hundreds of dollars for pets at stores, but not at shelters. When you adopt, you pay a small fee. Sometimes an adoption can even be free!

If you want a pet, visit a shelter. Try out adoption. You will make a lucky pet very happy!

How is getting a pet from an animal shelter different from getting a pet from a pet store? Circle a sentence that tells you.

Check off after each reading.

1st Reading

2nd Reading

3rd Reading

Comprehension Check

1. Reread page 248. What is the author's purpose for including information about life in shelters?

2. Reread page 249. How do the reasons on this page support the author's point?

3. Read this sentence.

   You can save a pet from an unhappy life. Give it a cozy, comfortable home!

   Write a sentence that tells how a real home could be *comfortable* for a pet.

Name: ______________________________

May I Suggest a Puppy?

1 1st Reading **Main Topic**

Main Topic
Page 226

Page 227	Page 228	Page 229

Name: ______________________________

May I Suggest a Puppy?

2 2nd Reading Author's Purpose

Page 227: The author wants to explain that ______________________________

______________________________.

Page 228: The author wants to explain that ______________________________

______________________________.

Page 230: The author wants to explain that ______________________________

______________________________.

3 3rd Reading Critical Thinking

Page 229: I can tell it is the author's opinion because

____

______________________________.

Page 230: Training forms a special bond between you and your puppy because

____

______________________________.

Name: ______________________________

Get an Older Dog!

1 1st Reading **Compare and Contrast**

Older Dogs	Both	Puppies
Page 238	**Page 236**	**Page 237**
Page 239		**Page 239**

Name: ______________________________

Get an Older Dog!

2 2nd Reading Support for Author's Points

Page 236: The author's opinion is that ______________________________

______________________________.

Page 238: These reasons support the point that ______________________________

____

______________________________.

Page 240: This reason supports the point that

____

______________________________.

3 3rd Reading Critical Thinking

Page 237: Puppies are too much work because ______________________________

______________________________.

Page 240: It is important for a dog to be gentle and peaceful because

____

______________________________.

Glossary

A

answer
a response to a question (Lessons 1, 4, 5)

author's purpose
the reason why the author wrote the text (Lessons 7, 8)

B

bold print
text that is darker than the text around it (Lesson 6)

C

caption
a phrase or a sentence that tells more about a drawing or a photograph (Lessons 6, 7)

central message
the main idea, lesson, image, or feeling in a story or poem that the writer wants you to understand (Lessons 2, 4)

character
a person or an animal in a story (Lessons 2, 3)

compare

to look at how two or more things are the same **(Lessons 1, 3, 6, 8)**

compound word

a word that is made up of two smaller words **(Lesson 3)**

EXAMPLE

bedtime, sunburn

connect ideas

read carefully to link one idea with another **(Lessons 5, 6)**

context clue

a word or words that help you figure out the meaning of a word you do not know **(Lessons 1, 5, 7)**

EXAMPLE

I brought my equipment. I brought a glove, a bat, and a ball.

contrast

to look at how two or more things are different **(Lessons 1, 3, 6, 8)**

D

diagram
a drawing that shows the parts of something or how something works **(Lessons 6, 7)**

dictionary
a book or a Web site that gives the meanings of words **(Lesson 1)**

drawing
an image that helps you better understand a text **(Lesson 7)**

F

fable
a story that teaches a lesson about life **(Lesson 2)**

folktale
a story that has been told and retold for a long time **(Lesson 3)**

G

glossary
a list of words and their meanings found at the end of some informational texts **(Lesson 5)**

I

illustration
a picture that you see in a story that helps you understand the events and characters **(Lessons 1, 3)**

inference
a good guess you make about something that an author does not tell you **(Lesson 4)**

L

label
a word that names a part of a diagram or other image **(Lesson 6)**

M

main topic
what an informational text is mostly about **(Lessons 5, 8)**

map
a picture that shows the different parts of a place, such as mountains, rivers, cities, towns, and streets **(Lesson 5)**

moral
the lesson or message that the author wants you to understand in a fable **(Lesson 2)**

multiple-meaning word
a word that has more than one meaning **(Lesson 7)**

O

opinion
what the author thinks or feels about a topic in a text **(Lesson 8)**

P

photograph
a picture that helps you better understand a text **(Lessons 5, 7)**

poet
a person who writes poetry **(Lesson 4)**

poetry
carefully chosen words that show ideas or feelings **(Lesson 4)**

point of view
how a person thinks or feels about something or someone **(Lesson 3)**

point
an idea that an author states to support his or her opinion **(Lesson 8)**

prefix
a word part that is added to the beginning of a root word **(Lessons 2, 6)**

EXAMPLE

unkind, reheat

process
a series of steps that take place to make or do something **(Lesson 7)**

Q

question
a sentence that asks for information **(Lessons 1, 4, 5)**

R

real-life connection
connecting a word or words you read to people or events in real life **(Lessons 4, 8)**

reason
an idea that an author includes to support a point **(Lesson 8)**

respond
to act, say, think, or feel something about events or challenges in a story **(Lessons 1, 2, 3)**

retell
to tell a story's beginning, middle, and end in your own words **(Lesson 2)**

rhythm
the beat or pattern of stress in a poem that is used to emphasize certain words and create meaning **(Lesson 4)**

root word
the main part of a word that tells the word's meaning **(Lessons 3, 7)**

S

science term
a word or phrase that is important for understanding a science topic **(Lesson 6)**

science text
a text with true information about a science topic **(Lesson 6)**

sequence
the order in which events happen (Lesson 5)

shades of meaning
words that tell about a similar idea or action, but that have slightly different meanings (Lessons 4, 8)

EXAMPLE

big, enormous, gigantic
hop, skip, jump

social studies text
a text with true information about real people, places, and events (Lesson 5)

story
made-up events with made-up characters (Lesson 1)

story structure
the parts of a story (the beginning, middle, and end) that work together to tell the story (Lessons 1, 2)

subhead
a title for a section of text (Lessons 6, 7)

suffix
a word part that is added to the end of a root word (Lesson 2)

EXAMPLE

fear<u>ful</u>, fear<u>less</u>

supporting paragraph
a paragraph that tells more about the main topic **(Lesson 8)**

T

technical text
a text that tells about how something works, how something is made, or how to do something **(Lesson 7)**

text feature
a special part of a text that makes it easier for readers to read and find information **(Lessons 6, 7)**

title
a name that tells what a text, diagram, or map is about **(Lesson 6)**

Acknowledgments

Poetry

"April Rain Song" From THE COLLECTED POEMS OF LANGSTON HUGHES by Langston Hughes, edited by Arnold Rampersad with David Roessel, Associate Editor, copyright © 1994 by The Estate of Langston Hughes. Permission granted by Alfred A. Knopf, an imprint of the Knopf Doubleday Publishing Group, a division of Random House LLC for print rights and by Harold Ober Associates Incorporated for electronic rights. All rights reserved.

"Keep a Poem in Your Pocket" From SOMETHING SPECIAL by Beatrice Schenk de Regniers. Copyright © 1958 Beatrice Schenk de Regniers. Copyright renewed 1986. Permission for print and electronic rights granted by Marian Reiner. All rights reserved.

"Rope Rhyme" Copyright © 1978 by Eloise Greenfield. Permission for print and electronic rights granted by HarperCollins Publishers. All rights reserved.

"We Have a Secret" Originally published with no title in 1915.

Photos 3: Brandon Alms; 4: (t)Eric Isselée, (b)adogslifephoto; 45: rgbdigital; 70: margouillatphotos; 77: Digital Vision; 80: Big Cheese Pictures; 87: yganko; 102: marcduf; 103: nicolas nadjar; 107: Sveta Demidoff; 110: Jupiterimages; 111: Photodisc; 115: monkeybusinessimages; 127: Gary Tognoni; 128: SusanSerna; 130: (b)TonyFeder, (t)Jami Garrison; 131: Tim_Lescinski; 132: Courtesy of the Library of Congress, LC-USZ62-52000; 133: Samson1976; 134: (r)National Park Service, (l)Hemera Technologies; 135: frontpoint; 138: Smileus; 140: Martin Rowe; 141: Mark Atkins; 142: Stockbyte; 143: Green Belt Movement; 144: (l)AP Photo/ Bjorn Sigurdson, (r)Wavebreakmedia Ltd.; 145: National Park Service; 148: Comstock; 149: DrPAS; 150: Courtesy of the Library of Congress, LC-USZ62-14802; 151: (t)Courtesy of the Library of Congress, LC-DIG-det-4a13059, (b)Courtesy of the Library of Congress, LC-DIG-ppmsca-08371; 153: (l)littleny, (r)marekuliasz; 159: Dynamicfoto-PedroCampos; 160: Elena Butinova; 162: (t)anankkml, (b)f9photos; 163: Robin_Kay; 165: (l)Crazybboy, (r)webguzs; 166: fazon1; 167: kurapy11; 170: Photos.com; 172: (t)almoond, (b)slkoceva; 174: Johnny Lye; 176: Wlad74; 180: Brandon Alms; 181: 1stGallery; 183: (t)GlobalP, (b)GlobalP; 184: Atelopus; 185: Megan Lorenz; 191: Wavebreakmedia Ltd; 192: HandmadePictures; 194: (t)Coprid, (b,l)anna1311, (b,r)Federico Rostagno; 195: (l)unclepodger, (r)Vasyl Kozub; 196: (t)millionsjoker, (b)ffolas; 197: (t,l)Serenethos, (b)SergeyChayko, (t,m)Maya Kovacheva Photography, (t,r)Pat_Hastings; 198: (l)Xebeche, (m)scanrail, (r)MIXA next; 202: Grafner; 204: (t)Eric Isselée, (l)Kroljaaa, (b,r)ClaudioVentrella, (b,l)Merih Unal Ozmen; 205: (l)Jaimie Duplass, (r)Tomas_Mina; 206: (l)belchonock, (r)Monkey Business Images; 207: (l)olgakr, (r)Tom Perkins; 208: Hung_Chung_Chih; 209: Patrick Heagney; 212: Elmik; 213: Catherine dée Auvil; 214: (far left, top to bottom)Dave King, Fesus Robert, Ingram Publishing, anna1311, Alex_str, Hemera Technologies, (middle left, top to bottom)anna1311, Elena Schweitzer, Alexlukin, Top Photo Corporation, Joy Fera, (middle right, top to bottom)Elena Schweitzer, atoss, Natikka, anna1311, ValentijnTempels, (far right, top to bottom) Ignasi Martin, nito100, caimacanul, suslik83, Nastco; 215: (l)bee_photobee, (r)mareandmare; 216: (t)Howard Shooter, (m,l)Let-c, (b,l)Top Photo Corporation, (b,m)Roksana Bashyrova, (m,r)AndreaAstes, (b,r)ValentijnTempels; 223: Fuse; 224: Denyshutter; 226: (t)Ingram Publishing, (m,l)Silense, (m,r)Elenathewise, (b)Jani Bryson; 227: (t)Ingram Publishing, (b)adogslifephoto; 228: (t)Ingram Publishing, (b)Kai Chiang; 229: (t)Ingram Publishing, (b)Huntstock; 230: (t)Ingram Publishing, (b)gurinaleksandr; 231: Maksimovairina; 234: CamiloTorres; 236: (b)LWA/Dann Tardif, (t)ma_rish; 237: Studio-Annika ; 238: AndraA Cerar; 239: Jupiterimages; 240: Jupiterimages; 241: OceanBodhi; 244: Zoonar RF; 245: (t)Roslen Mack, (b)cynoclub; 246: (t)Roslen Mack, (m,l)Salinde, (m,r)Thinkstock, (b)Eric Isselée; 247: (t)Roslen Mack, (m)Irina Karlova, (b)Fuse; 248: (t)Roslen Mack, (m)gaikphotos, (b)cynoclub; 249: (t)Roslen Mack, (b)Glenda Powers.

Illustrations 2: (t)Martina Pelusa, (b)Margeaux Lucas; 3: Amy Wummer; 5, 18, 19, 20, 21, 22: Laura Sua; 8, 9, 10, 11, 12, 106: Richard Hoit; 6: Tigatelu; 13: Aileen Denise Martin; 16: colematt; 23: graphic-bee; 26, 27, 28, 29, 30, 31: Hector Borlasca; 38: Glenne82; 2, 40, 41, 42, 43, 44: Martina Pelusa; 48: glowonconcept; 50, 51, 52, 53, 54: Woody Fox; 55: HitToon; 59, 60, 61, 62, 63, 72, 73, 74, 75, 76: Margeaux Lucas; 2, 82, 83, 84, 85, 86: David Shepherd; 91, 92, 93, 94, 95, 112-113: Jamie Smith; 104-105: Amy Wummer; 107: Sveta Demidoff; 114, 119: Susan Keeter; 120, 121: Tracey Bishop; 131, 135, 140, 152, 164, 173, 175, 199, 213, 217: Peter Bull; 150: AlexanderZam; 177: Dorling Kindersley.